www.exjwsupport.co.uk

ISBN:9798862018295

Thanks and so much to love to Helen,
the most amazing wife in the world.

WELCOME

An introduction from the author

This book is meant as a guide for all Jehovah's Witnesses and ex-Jehovah's Witnesses alike. The contents are from the personal experiences of many ex-Jehovah's Witnesses.

Everything in this book is based on my own personal viewpoint and opinion. I am not a professional counsellor, neither am I a historian, geologist, scientist, mathematician, religious scholar or academic. This book is one small opinion in an entire world history of opinions, wisdoms and philosophies. I can strongly advice never to listen or take on faith just one source of information, but to use as many different sources as possible.

If anything in this book causes distress, seek professional help and support. You are not alone in this journey. Just reach out.

Jonny Halfhead

@JonnyHalfhead

Credits
Jonny Halfhead – Writer, Graphics
Editor – Helen Leaper
Photographs – Helen Leaper, Jonathan Leaper, many images created through the AI engine DeepDreamGenerator and Unsplash.com

Designed on GIMP

CONTENTS

Faith to Faithless is a programme of Humanists UK which works to raise awareness of the issues faced by those who leave high-control religious groups and provide support to those affected. Deciding to leave a religion often means rejection from family and community, and the ex-religious may end up homeless, isolated, and at risk of abuse. In addition, many high-control religions prevent members from accessing education or external services, and so individuals don't know where to turn for support. We provide facilitated peer support groups and social groups, provide a platform for ex-religious voices to be heard, and raise awareness of the issues they face. We train statutory and support organisations like the police, social services, and mental health organisations to better understand the issues the ex-religious face, and the policy and practice implications this might have for them. We were founded in 2015. Now run by a staff team of three and advised by a voluntary Leadership Team of ex-religious people with lived experience, the programme has expanded its capacity to both support individuals and effect sustainable change.

SERVICES WE OFFER

- Weekly online peer support sessions run by trained facilitators.
- Monthly online social events for ex-religious LGBT people.
- Monthly online social events for ex-religious women.
- Regular in-person social events around the UK.
- Connecting people with psychotherapists.
- Limited free sessions with a psychotherapist who specialises in supporting those who leave controlling religions.
- Educational events that aim to correct the misinformation religions teach. For example, how life began, evolution, feminism, and so on.

We also have a Helpline that offers a listening ear, informal emotional support, and a way for the ex-religious to reduce their isolation. Or people can email if they prefer. You can call this number for free from all mobiles and landlines and it won't appear on itemised bills.

0800 448 0748

helpline@faithtofaithless.com

Purpose

Hello Reader

As I have always done with my books, I start to write and part way through I stop and get stuck in a loop of self-questioning, self-analysing and self-doubting until I come to a grinding halt because the same two big questions always crop up. What am I trying to accomplish by writing this book and who am I to be expressing myself and advising other people how to live their lives?

I've already hit these questions several times while simply trying to get this book started. As I look back on my life and the experiences I've had, both as a Jehovah's Witness and as a person who has lived even more time in the outside world, I've finally managed to get myself to a place where I can subjectively look back at both lives with some level of balance.

I came from a congregation of over one hundred and knew a couple of hundred more in nearby congregations. Since leaving I've met and talked to a similar number of ex Jehovah's Witnesses and have also met many diverse and different people in my life that know little to nothing of this unusual religion.

There is also one thing that I am finding out about myself, which seems to be quite rare in the community of former Jehovah's Witnesses, and that is that I only have a small amount of natural fear of my former peers left, an issue that can still wield power and influence over a person even decades after leaving.

A bit about myself.
I was born into the Jehovah's Witnesses religion. Both my parents and grandparents were Jehovah's Witnesses. I grew up in a very strict and religious environment. Soon after 1975, my father stopped attending the meetings and was eventually disfellowshipped when I was about seven years old, which was then followed by my parents getting divorced. We (my brother, sister and I) stayed with my mother as my father became homeless. My father then became painted as "an absent devil" who was to be cut out of all family memory and even physical photographs.

As a teenager I suffered heavily from bullying, blackouts and stress induced hallucinations while trying so very hard to be a good Jehovah's Witness in a tightly controlled and strict congregation in the middle of the English countryside. Although pressured to get baptised when all my friends around me were, I never succumbed. Despite this, in my late teenage years I was still disassociated and treated as disfellowshipped for several months after a very innocent sexual encounter with a girl. I was tarred and marked as a bad association for nearly three years until I was thrown out of my mother's house aged 19 and was left isolated, homeless and alone with a huge faith crisis and the abandonment of all my friends and family. It was under this cloud of loneliness that I tried to commit suicide.

Why Am I doing this book then?

I have been in that very dark place where everything seems lost and there seems to be no way out. I have also crawled out of that dark space only to find that my past follows me and the consequences of stress and trauma triggers make their way to the surface. Then I tried to forget my trauma, move on and try and forget what to me was a normal but stressful past life. I still then found even decades later that I could still be triggered and what I thought was behind me and finished with was still very raw and painful.

It was only then that I truly faced up to my past traumas and after therapy realised how much of an impact my Jehovah's Witnesses upbringing had on me and how much my past life was far from normal, that it was, in fact, extraordinary.

The organisation is at a critical point in history as I write this book in 2023. Many people are leaving the organisation and find themselves in the same dark and confusing place that I was in decades ago. Thankfully, there is now a lot more support out there on the internet for people leaving the Jehovah's' Witnesses organisation. There is a lot of support in groups and forums from people that have suffered the same trauma and are willing to help.

There are also lots of things to learn afresh when you leave the Jehovah's Witness organisation and the amount of information and the number of sources of guidance and support can seem overwhelming at times. When leaving the Jehovah's witnesses, you can also be very vulnerable to suggestion, or can be desperate to make up for lost time, or may not even know all of the unusual events of the organisation from the past hundred years.

I hope to give you a few pointers of what I have learned along my journey so it may be of use to you, not as another way of controlling your life but as a voice of experience that can at least help you see your situation in a different way or from a different angle. That is why I want to reiterate that everything in this book is written from my own personal experience and your experience might not be the same, but hopefully you might find some of the contents useful in your own personal journey.

This is as far away from an instruction manual as it is possible to get. It's a collection of experiences and viewpoints that has taken me over three decades to formulate since leaving the Jehovah's Witnesses. Other former witnesses will likely have totally contrary viewpoints.

The positive side of your newfound freedom is that you are free to research as many sources of wisdom, guidance and information as you can, which is the best way to form an opinion, after comparing many conflicting arguments.

Nothing I say in this book is absolute fact, it is just my opinion. You may think that some of the things I have to say are totally wrong. That is the beauty of freedom. You can go and do your own research, prove me wrong, disagree and form your own opinion. Just try to do it after doing your own research. Don't believe something I say just because I have published it in a book.

You are on a fascinating journey, because you will discover so many new and interesting things. As you learn, I will warn you to not get bogged down in regret. You had a former life where you did the best with the experience and wisdom you had and in the same circumstances, without the wisdom of hindsight, you would probably make the same decisions again and again.

So try not to be regretful, accept your former life and use it as fuel to improve your life now. Wisdom comes from lessons learned, so you have the opportunity for great wisdom if you let your experiences guide you on a path of improvement.

"That is the beauty of freedom. You can go and do your own research"

Do what is right for you.

When leaving the Jehovah's Witnesses there is no right or wrong way to do it. You have the opportunity to forge your own path and as long as you don't intend to hurt anyone, there is no right or wrong way.

That statement on its own we already know is loaded and heavy. Your friends and family will say that you are hurting them greatly by leaving the organisation and therefore leaving them. From an outsider's perspective, this seems such an upside down view of that inner world.

As someone that has seen both inside and outside the organisation, I know that there is little that I can say to persuade you that the people inside the organisation are in greater danger then everyone else outside of it.

Those poor people still stuck in the organisation don't want to see the dangers that lurk in the midst of the congregation. You are safer outside of that control and manipulation and there is hope that your actions may persuade others to question their situation.

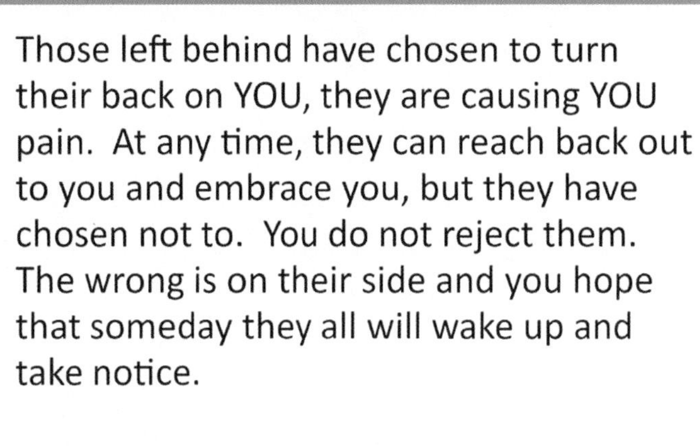

> **"I do not at all believe in human freedom in the philosophical sense. Everybody acts not only under external compulsion but also in accordance with inner necessity."**
> **Albert Einstein**

Those left behind have chosen to turn their back on YOU, they are causing YOU pain. At any time, they can reach back out to you and embrace you, but they have chosen not to. You do not reject them. The wrong is on their side and you hope that someday they all will wake up and take notice.

Saying that, only YOU can decide how, or even if, you should leave. The ex-Jehovah's Witnesses community collectively have a group of acronyms for the different mental states of those in and out of the organisation. These can only be self-diagnosed, truthfully. Some people may show outward signs of being devoted and yet in their actions, desire for power, bullying, harassment and greed, in reality show how true they really are to their professed faith. But these people usually think they are totally devoted still.

Four States Of Mind

PIMI – Physically In Mentally In.
Those that believe that they are totally devoted to the Jehovah's Witnesses' organisation, totally committed mentally and spiritually to it.

PIMO – Physically In Mentally Out.
A very difficult place to be. Knowing that something is very wrong with the organisation and yet continuing to show all outward signs of being devoted to it. Going to meetings, doing the ministry and studying.

Many people still get baptised while in this state because of the peer pressure and fear of what will happen if they don't, not because they truly desire to get baptised. The fear of leaving and being shunned by family, friends and your whole community can be a horrible place to be, so a person tows the line. It is well known that huge swathes of current Jehovah's Witnesses currently fit this mental state and are trapped inside.

POMI – Physically Out Mentally In.
Many times, someone will be disfellowshipped and that person can be longing and working to get back into the congregation and to be accepted once again.
A portion of people that "wake up" and leave the organisation, can spend many years, even decades, desiring to be back in the perceived safety of the congregation, regretting their decision to leave. Many will profess to have left it all behind but will still carry regret, their indoctrination will give them doubts that leaving was the right thing to do. There are many stories of people drifting back in even after decades away. POMI describes that mental state.

POMO – Physically Out Mentally Out.
Those that have been able to openly confront their trauma, find rehabilitation and can see without anger, how insignificant Jehovah's Witnesses are in the world.
Only when you truly see how unimportant the whole religion and its controlling state is and how it holds no real power or influence except for that which you give it, do you truly become free.

Many see the organisation for what it is and lose faith in it, yet find that the threat of losing their entire reality, family, friends, colleagues and the perceived warmth of the congregation can be too much to bear. So, they walk the tightrope that is PIMO. It is the hardest thing to do, to live two lives and hope that you can keep up the pretences. But nobody can tell you how to live your life. If this how you choose to cope, then that is your choice.

I'll say again, there is no right or wrong way. Be wary though that this is the most difficult state to maintain. Yet it can be a good thing. Your eyes might be unveiled to the reality of what the organisation is and that can only positively influence others still trapped inside the congregation. You can have more effect on friends and family in the congregation from within than you can ever have if shunned and excommunicated and living on the outside.

Only you can know what is right for you. How you choose to leave or stay, is your right, your freedom of choice. But you do need to look after your mental health while in this difficult place and this is another reason why being PIMO is very difficult.

"Only you know what is right for you."

The witnesses profess to believe in the collective and not the self. They teach that the sin of the world is in its selfishness. But in order to heal, you need to look after yourself in some way. The problem is that the organisation has drilled into you that thinking for your self is selfish and self-centred, that thinking of yourself takes away the ability to think for others and for god.

The Jehovah's Witnesses environment is full of black and white and life just isn't that simple. They teach you that you will either be humble or narcissistic and nothing in-between. They teach that looking after oneself is totally narcissistic and evil.

And yet, think about when you go on holiday and fly on a plane. Before take-off, the stewards give you instructions about how to put on your oxygen mask in an emergency. They instruct you to put on your own mask first before that of your child or anyone else around you. That's because if you don't look after your basic needs first, you won't be in any state to help anyone else.

This is just one of the reasons why Jehovah's Witnesses are actually quite harmful. If you don't look after your own mental welfare, you cannot be in any fit state to help anyone else out. Looking after yourself does not mean that you will be filled with a flood of self-satisfaction and will lose your personality in a freefall of selfish driven, intent to walk all over everyone you know from then on. It doesn't work like that. You should heal yourself first so that then you can heal others.

The organisation uses your low self-esteem to control you and keep you always questioning your own ability to reason and question. It's one of the hallmarks of a cult I'm afraid. If you look after your own mental health, it's inevitable that at some

"If you don't look after your own mental welfare, you cannot be in any fit state to help anyone else out."

point you will have the strength to ask questions and stand up for yourself and the organisation believes that is not required for devotion to god.

Don't underestimate the spiritual impact either questioning or leaving the Jehovah's Witnesses will have on your life. While being an active Jehovah's Witness, you will have had the luxury of being given a completed set of moral and spiritual values all put together for you and wrapped up in a seemingly complete and neat doctrinal package. As your eyes open, you will find many problems with this package. You may have already noticed many holes and kinks in the supposed perfect code of morals and behaviours.

People who leave the organisation, naturally react differently to the hypocrisy they have discovered. Some react almost drunkenly to a newfound freedom away from the myriad of rules, written and unwritten. Many feel euphoric and free. Some feel angry and deeply bitter. All these reactions are understandable. In those moments though, like a tightly compacted spring being released, many people throw all moral and spiritual boundaries away and soon find themselves either doing things they regret in the future or then struggle to retract and rediscover their spiritual centre ever again.

Take some time to reflect and dwell upon your loss of predefined boundaries and try to get a sense of what you really want from life, which is not an easy thing to do when faced with losing your religion. It's a perfectly natural reaction to become atheist in response to what you have seen and witnessed. The same can be said for instantly looking for another religion to try and fill the void as soon as possible. The key is being aware of the trauma to your life and being conscious of what is happening and attempt to just slow down a little and take stock.

Your moral compass will be severely challenged and finding you have no rules to live by other than those which you decide upon can quickly throw you down the road of partying, drinking, drugs and sex (if you're lucky).

There's nothing wrong with any of this as far as your personal choices go, that is the gift of freedom. Just make sure that you consciously make those decisions and don't just fall into subconscious reactions that could affect the rest of your life.

Another pattern noticed by most after they leave the organisation is that they take their programmed mental state with them. You will likely find yourself constantly questioning and over thinking everything in your life. So, while I advise being aware of your situation and not being too rash in following your subconscious, also be aware of your indoctrinated over-analysing of everything. It's a trait that I have carried for decades, and it can be a huge setback when trying to fit in socially or when trying to be mentally positive in one's outlook.

I always find it best to have someone to talk to about moral and spiritual things. That's one of the advantages of the Ex-Jehovah's Witnesses community as they can help you talk some of these issues through. Sometimes an idea or a moral stance sounds good in your head, its only when it is verbalised that it might sound ridiculous or extreme.

...from those that know

"Since leaving Jehovah's Witnesses and following the work I now do to alert others of the hidden dangers within, I have often been asked "Why not just go quietly and get on with life?".

What motivates someone to use every opportunity to highlight their faults and lies? It comes from one of the most powerful driving forces that exist – Justice.

Having been lied to, deceived and worse, experienced sexual abuse myself and other close family members at the hands of Jehovah's Witnesses, it demands shouting out that this is not the loving caring all-embracing crowd they claim to be. Rather a self-centred organisation that puts reputation before the interests of humans. It is finally being called out.

At recent High Court cases, the Watchtower lawyers called me a "disgruntled elder". There is a lot to be disgruntled about! I am proud to be such, bringing attention to their deceitful false religious dogma."

John Viney
Ex-Jehovah's Witness Elder and now public activist for the rights of the abused and oppressed.

Martin Riley

Riley is a former Jehovah's Witness and anti-cult activist. He was raised in the Jehovah's Witness religion from childhood but was "disfellowshipped" (excommunicated) in 2019 at the age of 42. Although no longer active in the religion, he remained a believer until June 2020 when he decided to research the religion (using independent sources) for the very first time. After quickly realising that he'd been raised in a high-control doomsday cult, he started sharing his experiences of "waking up" from his religious indoctrination. Riley is now an outspoken advocate for people who've been affected by harmful religious practices and indoctrination. He has a YouTube channel called Jexit 2020 where he interviews fellow cult-survivors and debunks Jehovah's Witness doctrine.

Reflection

Recognising our own mental state

Fear

Fear controls us all. We need to respect how much it can shape everything about us. It makes us angry. Forces us to react in ways we wouldn't do without it. It can also protect us. But it can take over our personality to the point that our whole life can be controlled by it and you may not even initially recognise how much.
Fear is one of the main weapons of the Jehovah's Witnesses organisation. You fear that you will never be good enough, never pleasing Jehovah enough. You fear gossip and ridicule in the congregation when you aren't righteous enough. You fear the Elders and the power and control they have over you.

You fear Armageddon or fear losing the chance for ever lasting life. You fear letting down your family, bringing reproach on your family, letting down your friends, giving the organisation a bad name, having the congregation be ashamed of you. Most importantly you fear the loss of everything you know, your entire reality if you leave the organisation or question its truth or authority. The threat of losing your family, all your friends and your whole support network. The threat of losing that convenient, self-contained package of beliefs and morals that have been made and wrapped up in an unquestionable parcel has a huge impact on your future decisions.

Then, of course, we have been fed the myth about the outside world. We fear the danger of the unknown world outside filled with all those evil people that we feel safe and protected from when inside the congregation. One of the regular comments I hear from ex-Jehovah's Witnesses is the shock of how nice people are in the outside world. The world outside is no different from the world inside. There is a mixture of personalities. There are dangerous, violent, greedy, lying people on the outside, but there are those people on the inside as well and they are usually attracted to the power that certain positions in the organisation grant them. Most people in the outside world are good people just like in the congregation. The only real shock with some people on the

Fear can stop you from doing what you need to do in order to be mentally healthy. You may think that you do not have the power to overcome your fears, but you are much stronger than you think. You can help to minimise fear in several ways. Recognising it is the first step. Realising that your environment uses your fear to control you, can in itself, give you fuel to fight back against it.
Knowledge helps greatly. The more you learn, the more your fear can be controlled.

An animal when young can be taught discipline and fear. Many times, you can see cruelty inflicted on an Elephant and you look on and wander why the elephant with its huge size and massive power doesn't just turn around and use that against its human oppressor. It's usually because they have fear drilled into them when they are young, when the human master can inflict pain and dominate the animal whilst it is small. The elephant then carries that fear of humans through its adult life and still fears the same pain and trauma it felt from being young, despite its huge size. You have been conditioned in the same way, to fear people that have absolutely no power over you. They have taught you and drilled into you fears and stories that you will likely find are not the truths you thought they were.

When you eventually acquire the maturity of external wisdom, you will wonder how you were ever convinced to allow that fear and power to be put upon you.
There is also an intellectual and emotional maturity you will reach, where you may come to realise that to be part of a society that wants to live forever in paradise, would mean the biggest genocide in the history of humanity. That is what Armageddon actually is, mass genocide. You will also come to release that your reality is not what you thought it was. You will be born with new eyes and what you see will help alleviate that fear.
The fear of losing one's friends and family is very real. That is where your fear is warning you productively. Only you can decide what course of action is best for you in trying to keep your friends and family close. Friends will be made outside of the organisation. You will need to be patient and you will find that the friends on the outside are more likely to not put conditions on your friendship like those in the congregation do.

As for your family, only you can decide what you are able to cope with. Bear in mind though, that there might already be many secretly questioning the organisation, even within your family. If they see you leave, it might give them enough support and encouragement for them to leave knowing that you are on the outside waiting with open arms for them. You may also have family that you can now go and seek out if they were disfellowshipped or faded some time before.

You will also find that you fear words. Jehovah's Witness have their own use of language, just like any closed community does. Many of the words they use, carry specific fears and different uses of the spoken language. Understanding the re-interpretation of some of those words can help give you back power to confront why those words hold such power over you.

Anger

Anger is a natural response. It can be useful to give you the power to combat your fear. It can give you the energy to polarise and to get up and do something constructive. It can also eat into you, run like acid through your veins and destroy your life. Recognising the spectre of anger is your first step to controlling it.
It's more than understandable to be angry as a former Jehovah's Witness. It's not until you leave the Jehovah's Witness organisation that you truly begin to see the extent of the suffering the organisation has caused. The number of unregistered cases of child abuse worldwide are coming to the surface in the tens of thousands. Rapes, spousal abuse, drunkenness and violence are so commonplace that you will be shocked at how normal all these are, sitting just under the polished veneer of the congregation. You might very well have been a victim of one of these atrocities. They are endemic.

You will learn of these as you speak to other ex-Jehovah's Witnesses. Sometimes you may find it difficult to consolidate the shared experience of others with your experiences, but they are very real. You may wonder after you do more research on the organisation, how you never saw all these signs while on the inside. You may feel very betrayed when you see the physical evidence of governing body members lying under oath in a court of law on a live video feed. Like a constant barrage you will be hit with triggers of your former trauma even if, as yet, you do not see your time as one of Jehovah's Witnesses as traumatic. As triggers and reminders hit you, it's a natural reaction to feel more and more angry.

There can also be an intellectual hit. You may see yourself as a reasonably intelligent person and yet as you do your research, you will wonder how you didn't see all the things you will discover about the organisation. You will hear plenty of people say how they would never be duped into following any religion and would definitely never fall for the lure of a cult. There is a general attitude that only stupid people or the desperate would ever join any manipulating group.

This couldn't be further from the truth. It is usually those with intellect that seek out other beliefs, theories and philosophies of reality. It is in these arenas that predators lay and lie. If intelligence was a combatant to control and manipulation, then internet Spamming wouldn't be one of the biggest worldwide scourges of our time.

Any ex-Jehovah's Witness has an overabundance of reasons to be angry and bitter. Yet, apart from it being a useful positive fuel to improve and drive you to progress and to help others, it can also be very self-destructive and you can easily fall into yet another trap of control and manipulation. Anger will drive you to feedback your fear back onto yourself and you will begin to harm yourself and others if that anger is left unchecked.

One of the biggest weapons the Jehovah's Witness organisation uses is fear. One of those main fears is of the outside world. Years will have been spent drilling into you this picture of the outside world of sex, violence, filth and anger. You will find that this is mostly lies used to keep those stuck inside its controlling grasp. The worst thing we can do, for the sake of our former friends and our loved ones still stuck inside its prison, is fuel those very fears by giving them proof to back up the organisations lies.

Your anger will feed those lies and keep your loved ones trapped in fear. If they see you angry, they will assume it's because the "world's" influence has turned you that way. If you protest violently, it will reinforce everything the organisation says about apostates. If you shout out to them in the street, jump up on the platform in a Kingdom Hall or display any anger towards any current Jehovah's Witness, you add an extra barrier into the structure of protection they think they need in order to keep safe away from you. Your anger is fully justified and understandable from the outside, but for those on the inside, any display of anger strengthens their fear, which in turn strengthens the hold the organisation has on them.

So how do you convince your loved ones still stuck in "the truth" of the trap they are stuck in. Only love can really do it. If all they see from you is love and concern, if every time they hear from you or see you, you let them know you are waiting for them, that will open their eyes. You can disprove everything they fear, through love. Those stuck on the inside believe that shunning is a loving way to bring you back. But lack of anger and open love can give them a lifeline to the outside world. If your moral goodness, love and humility is greater than that shown on the inside, those who think themselves as moral and good would have to question what they see around them in the organisation.
That doesn't mean that it is bad to demonstrate against the Jehovah's Witnesses organisation. It doesn't mean that you don't have a right to legally pursue and punish someone who abused you. In fact, both can be demonstrations of love. Standing outside a Jehovah's Witness convention, if done with love and peace can help disprove the fear of those seeing you and what they believe about apostates. It could save someone's life and rescue them from the confines of their prison. Taking an offender to court can stop that person from damaging anyone else and show people both outside the organisation what some Jehovah's Witnesses are capable of and may also open the eyes of loved ones still stuck inside the organisation.

"Your anger will feed those lies and keep your loved ones trapped in fear"

Anger is nearly always a reaction to one's own lack of control, a frustration with oneself because of that lack of control or an annoyance with oneself that you could have done something differently in the past had you have known. Don't let your anger control you like the organisation and the people in it have done to you for years. Don't give the organisation the fuel it needs to promote fear. Find help. Direct it back at them in a way that has the highest impact, by returning love, justice and enlightenment to those still suffering.

Reality

You were living in a world that you thought you knew. You knew about the past, had a full grasp on history. Sure, there might have been a few things that didn't always make sense, but then that was where faith came in. You knew what was going to happen in the future. At least the next thousand years and more. Some of you would have been sure that you were going to live forever. Some of us like myself, never felt good enough to be going to paradise, so were convinced of their coming demise at Armageddon.

You had an entire world created for you and you were convinced of that entire reality. Only now you see that reality crumbling around you.

Don't underestimate how much of an impact that is going to have on your life. I was born into the Jehovah's Witnesses. Nearly all of my extended family lived in it. Why would I ever question anything that my peers, teachers and mentors told me about every aspect of that world around me.

Now you face uncertainty and will have, to some extent, to rebuild what reality is for you all over again. It's natural to take the majority of what you have learned with you on that journey and every time you find something in the universe that's not as you expected, it hurts as though a knife is slicing a part of you away.

In my twenties I formed my own rock band. I had to call the band Personality Crisis because I had lost so much of myself after losing my reality from the Jehovah's Witnesses and then a relationship stripped what was left of my fragile persona away from me. In the twenty years I was a Jehovah's Witness I was totally devoid of any true personality. It was as though I was only allowed one personality and that was the personality of the good Witness and nothing else. All sense of self was inhibited. No style, no choices, no freedom.

Everything I did seemed to end up with a chat from the Elders or from other peers in the congregation, even down to the music I listened to and the books I read.

> **"Question everything and don't be afraid of information, no matter where it comes from. Any group or organisation who tells you not to independently research them has something to hide. And anyone who tries to stop you from thinking is not your friend."**
>
> **Martin Riley – Mr Jexit, YouTuber**

You too may have problems trying to work out who you are. One minute you are in an environment where you are told who to be, what to think, what to look at, what to read, what not to do about every aspect of your life. In many ways it gives you a protective covering, an abstinence from responsibility because none of it is your fault, it's what you were told to do. If you are out from under that protection, you are solely responsible for your actions, you will have to make all those decisions for yourself.

Sometimes I completely understand how satisfying it is to let an invisible and mythological being take all the responsibility for one's decisions. In that respect it is a far easier and simpler life. But outside of that protection, you have to decide what you want from life and decide who you are going to be. To be suddenly presented with a whole universe of possibilities to choose from and the responsibility to rest solely on your own shoulders is a huge burden. Then, of course, you need to throw in the fact that you will be doing all that from outside that protective bubble, in a world you likely know little or absolutely nothing about. Then, you may feel the need to fit in somewhere else or just to fit in with the outside world that you are now a part of so that you don't look as vulnerable as you feel. The crisis of personality is an area of leaving the Jehovah's Witnesses that many ex-Jehovah's Witnesses don't talk about too much, but it is at the core of your battle to survive.

While trying to work all this inner turmoil out, you will probably be trying to work out how the outside world works and how you fit into it. You may also be having a crisis of faith on top of your struggles with your own personality. Faith in the dictionary is defined as "complete trust or confidence in someone or something". The word doesn't just been spiritual faith, it can also mean the believe we have in our peers. The problem is with our faith, is that we have trusted an organisation full of peers and the truth they told us.

Our parents, friends, Elders, congregation, Overseers, Branch Committees and Governing Body are all people we had faith in and trusted their advice, guidance and rules. That's before you even go into the more spiritual aspect of faith, from a god, Jesus, the angels and spirits.

Depending on where you are on your journey, you may have lost some or all faith in many of these. Your gut instinct may be to never trust anyone or anything ever again and to remove faith completely from your life. But you may not notice how much you need faith to function.

From birth you are taught and trained. As an infant it is natural to just accept what you are told or shown. You have to, because to develop would be impossible if you questioned every single thing you were told. Your ability to question depends a lot on the reaction to your questions. I remember asking that constant question "why" when I was a child and getting on my mother's nerves with it. A negative reaction from your peers can have a big influence on your ability to question. I got fed up with asking "why" because I never got any real answers.If you had to confirm everything that was said to you with proof or with experiment, you wouldn't be alive.

A parent tells you not to put your hand in the fire, for the sake of self-preservation you have to take a leap of faith and not try to prove the concept by experiment. When you are shown the light switch on the wall that lights up the bulb in the room, you don't feel the need to rip out the wiring from the wall to try and prove to yourself that the switch is connected to that one lightbulb and something else isn't at play. If we lived that life, we would never be able to grow past our infancy as there wouldn't be enough time in our lifespan to prove everything with certainty.

Thankfully as human beings we are lazy and willing to take the word of our peers that the truth we see around us is as explained to us throughout our lives.

We have believed everyone. Our parents, our teachers, our friends, our peers, our Elders and the printed words of the Governing Body.

It's so easy to replace one set of peers with another. We see and respect authority and automatically assume that everyone that provides us with information has truth in their heart and have only good intentions. Just because I have taken the time to write this book, does not mean I am right or correct in anything I say. You have the freedom to find out for yourself and draw your own conclusions. The advice I would wish you to consider, is using caution in all matters of faith, "truth" and "fact". Everyone has their own version of fact and just like the persuasion of the Governing Body, many people will have convincing arguments.

Personally, I believe in evolution. But I'm also lazy and haven't spent a lifetime studying and theorising the concept. I have taken it on faith that other people have spent a lifetime studying and know what they are talking about. Yet, I'm also aware that the majority of a scientist's time has been spent studying other people's theories and findings and they have taken many things on faith from them. They have to, simply because the field is so large that one lifetime is not enough to experiment and conclude everything for oneself. And then, just to complicate matters, many things are theories, based on theories, based on theories. All sound and logical theories, but theories after all. Layers and layers of faith build up while learning, to then progress that learning with experimentation, which is then peer reviewed and presented to you to take on faith or spend your whole lifetime to come to the possible same conclusion.

Then, of course, popularity and politics play a part in the building of "fact" and "truth". For years homosexuality in nature was covered up and obscured, because political thinking of the time was that homosexuality was completely unnatural and not to be found in nature anywhere. That it is a man-made concept. Now we know that to be completely untrue and that homosexuality is the social binder in many groups of animals with higher intelligence. Science was central to the political drive of the Nazi's who drove many routes of scientific thinking to back up their hatred of the Jews, of the euthanasia of the sick and disabled and the purity of the German people's race. An entire country of people had faith in their leaders and the "truth" that they gave them.

"An entire country of people had faith in their leaders..."

People who spend their lifetime studying and believing one set of "facts", feel more compelled to persuade you that their studies are truthful because of the harrowing consequences of a life wasted if they are wrong. Also, politicians use either religion or science, manipulated to their own agenda, to influence certain beliefs to be popular so that particular ways of thinking can be made acceptable and, therefore, profitable to certain small groups of people with power. The faith of popularity is the hardest to see through. The argument usually being "how can all these people be wrong?"

So how do you get through this minefield? Make up your own mind. Find your own way. Don't let anyone else take that journey for you. Never be shamed into changing your thinking and yet always be willing to change your mind. There's a quote from one of my favourite films that a doctrine can never be changed, but an idea always moves and develops. Develop an idea, not a doctrine.

As humans we are very conceited. We constantly like to pretend that what we know is definitive and set in stone, that we observe absolute facts and those that do not have our knowledge are somehow less than we are. And yet, Albert Einstein is famously quoted as saying "the more I learn, the more I realise how much I don't know" and the Greek philosopher Socrates said "I know that I know nothing".

We are poorly adapted creatures for the world around us. We have such limited inputs. The visible light we see is just one type of electromagnetic radiation, and the visible light spectrum is a tiny part (0.0035%) of the much bigger electromagnetic spectrum. We hardly see anything of the world around us. We can relate only to what we see and touch. Our brain has taught itself to ignore what it doesn't perceive as real by deciding on a world we experience by touch. There may be many things we don't register as seeing in our brains because we filter out so much "noise" from our eyes. Then, in our conceit, we base our faith, our doctrine and our dogma on "fact" based on these filtered limited inputs and ridicule anyone else that doesn't share the same beliefs.

If you ever have the time, have a search online for Plato's Allegory of the cave. It is an interesting "reflection" on how limited we are as humans when it comes to truly seeing the world around us. I have often thought of the Jehovah's Witnesses as a large group of people all stuck at the bottom of the same wishing well. They have created this world of stone and mortar around them which protects them but also isolates them. This dark world, where exposure to the outside is limited to a narrow band of light a long way up the cold wet clammy stone walls, is the only proper view of the outer world. From their relative safety at the bottom of that wishing well, everyone forms a collective opinion of what the outside world is really like. Of course, a world view is highly unlikely to be accurate from such an observational position and yet the Jehovah's Witnesses insist on trying to tell everyone else by shouting up the funnel to anyone that will listen, what the world outside is like and how wonderful it is to be stuck at the bottom of that dark well with everyone else that is in the same predicament. It is impossible for them to have a proper world view.

I, personally, have come to feel very sorry for those still trapped down the bottom of that wishing well in the dark, the cold and the damp. They are very sure of the love and warmth of their fellow brothers and sisters trapped down there with them. They fear what they do not know or understand outside. They could climb out, but they would leave behind the world they know and leave their family and their friends. Trapped down that wishing well with everyone else is a ruling class of people that, through their own fear of what lies above ground, convince everyone else around them that only death and pain are outside the safe confines of that dark, damp well. They are all trapped in fear of what lies beyond that small circle of light. Then a whole fictional fantasy is built up about the reality of the outside world based on such limited exposure to it. A fantasy is created to keep loved ones from escaping and running away. It takes very little knowledge to realise how much that limited world view is skewed and built purely for control.

View from the Outside

"I guess the advice I'd give my younger self would be that you don't need to be afraid and feel so much guilt and pressure. That I am worthy of love that is without conditions.
Art has been my voice when words could not be said, my wings when they were torn, my escape, my healing."
Riches Road – Artist

One significant thing that sometimes takes years to learn once outside, is how insignificant the Jehovah's Witnesses are in the outside world. The organisation teaches us that god's work is so important, that knowledge of Jehovah and his organisation will reach the whole world triggering the end of the end, Armageddon. Many of us carry that conceit with us even when we leave the organisation behind.
You will find that hardly anyone knows anything about the Jehovah's Witnesses. Some will know them as the ones that knock on your door, but then so do Mormons, charity workers, salespeople and conmen. Some might have seen the carts on the street. But ask people what they know about the Jehovah's Witnesses and they barely know that they exist and have no idea what they are about or what they believe in or do. And that is from the veneer of the western world, where Christianity is already the norm and so Jehovah's Witnesses are just another denomination. The rest of the world are mostly oblivious to the presence of Jehovah's Witnesses.

Strangely the organisation would have us all believe that the preaching work reaches every corner of the globe, that they are at the forefront of ridicule and oppression everywhere. They give the impression that everyone in the world has heard and knows about the message that Jehovah's Witnesses are working so very hard to get out to the world and to save. But that is a massive over exaggeration.

The "message" is not as prolific as you think, it hardly gets told in the world at all. In a western country such as the UK, there is a higher concentration of Jehovah's Witnesses per population than in most countries. In the UK hardly anything is known about what Jehovah's Witnesses believe. Nobody outside the organisation knows why they try and convert people. Even relatives of Jehovah's Witnesses have no clue as to why they try so hard to push their religion on them. And yet we are to believe that the world is being given the chance to know what god is going to do before the biggest mass genocide is to take place at Armageddon.

If you do step out into the outside world, if you manage to climb up the sheer wall of that damp wishing well and clamber out of the darkness, there will likely be a few things about the outside world that you may not know or won't fully appreciate.

For instance, the world outside is not one big orgy of sexual depravity. Sure, if you want to, you can find pockets of it, in very specialised circles of society, but it's not everywhere. Jehovah's Witnesses would have you believe that all people do in the outside world is have sex, constantly. You may have been told that all nightclubs are just full of loud music, flashing strobe lights and open, rampant orgies. You may believe that every weekend, everyone in the world goes out to bars purely to have sex with anyone and everyone. I'm sorry to say that just isn't the case. People in the world are just as prudish and hung up about public displays of sex and nudity as people are in the congregation. In fact, you might find that there are more sex scandals per capita in the organisation than there is on the outside. That's probably due to heavy censorship and sexual oppression.

Masturbation might be seen as harmless out in the world generally, but no-one will talk about it, it's still taboo as a subject even though everyone is free to do what they please. Oh, and by the way, masturbation is not bad for you. You won't catch diseases, you won't burn alive for it, it doesn't turn you into a psychopath and a myriad of other ridiculous fables and myths about the pursuit of something that is very common and natural to do.

The outside world is also trying to come out from a few Victorian hangovers as regards the power of the sexes, race, gender and sexual orientation. You might find that initially you unintentionally take some of your prejudices with you from being a Jehovah's Witness. The world outside is very sensitive to matters of race, gender, skin colour and culture. Now you may think that Jehovah's Witnesses are not racist at all, but that depends on where your congregation is located and how exposed it is to such issues. You will find as well that the Jehovah's Witness organisation is not as clean cut as you think and that some prejudice will certainly follow you on your journey of discovery. The publications of Jehovah's Witnesses never show anyone of colour or even any women when depicting either angels, heavenly people or spirits. The remnant might be made up of black or female people while on the earth, but all the literature of the organisation shows them as white, male and having beards once they get to heaven. This is deeply insulting once you see and notice it.

Jehovah's Witnesses are also culturally racist when it comes to other faiths and religions. There is no respect whatsoever for any other faith or belief. They are all part of Babylon The Great. No matter how spiritual or good a person is, if they don't worship the god of the Jehovah's Witnesses then they are evil and bad. And it seems the further east you go with religion and beliefs, the greater the evil that faith and belief system is. Be aware of carrying that racism with you into the outside world. Not everyone in the outside world is trying to stand to a higher moral stance with these issues, but there is at least a general progression by society to try and be better and to improve as a civilisation.

Another difference in the outside world is getting used to the equality of sex. The Jehovah's Witnesses are very patriarchal, even though they try and deny it outwardly and publicly. In the outside world there is an ongoing struggle to make the sexes equal. You will find that you automatically bring a sexist prejudice with you. You may believe that women are weaker, more emotional, that they use and manipulate men. You may even believe, as many Elders do when disciplining sexual matters in the congregation, that a woman uses her attractiveness and sexuality to lure men into doing things a man would never do without the sexual power that women use.

I have heard this story so many times, over and over again from former Jehovah's Witnesses, that Elders have accused

Gabriela Staniszewska – Ex-Jehovah's Witness

"I would advise [anyone now leaving the Jehovah's Witnesses] to educate themselves on high-control organisations and cult tactics.

This was one of the most powerful tools that helped me personally to come to terms with the fact that I was a victim of a massive scam called "Watch Tower Bible and Tract Society of Pennsylvania", and that I had been duped.

Also, research, research, research. Once you allow yourself to learn and to trust information about history, biology, geology, anthropology, psychology and compare what you learned with the JWs teachings, you will realise that they have created almost an alternative reality where truth and facts are distorted to fit their own ideology.

Learning that what I was taught by my parents from the age of 8 and what I believed to be the one and only absolute truth was actually a lie and everything I did believe wasn't real was very traumatic. I would advise everyone leaving high-control organisations such as JWs to seek professional help and go through therapy.

I've been in therapy for almost two years now and I honestly don't know how I'd have coped without it immediately after leaving and in the months after. Indoctrination, mind control, constant women of inviting sex, encouraging rape by provocation, that a women must have secretly desired to be assaulted because she didn't scream and say no. I have also talked to people that have had this said to them as children about an older man, that they must have encouraged or invited molestation. This is, unfortunately, one of the sicknesses inside the Jehovah's Witnesses organisation that you may not yet realise.

The sexes are equal in an equal society that we all in the world outside are trying to make better, while battling against this byproduct of religion and a lesser educated society which civilisation is still trying to move away from. It is too easy for anyone coming from the organisation to drop into old habits when it comes to these matters. It is important to check your manners regularly to make sure that those deeply ingrained prejudices don't just affect the way you interact with others, but how you perceive yourself. It's so easy to come out of the organisation still underestimating your own ability and right as a human to not only exist but even flourish. Many of us bring these inbuilt biases and still inflict them on ourselves.

An important part of getting over an inbuilt brainwashing is overriding the perception that gay people are evil, immoral, unnatural and mentally diseased. The outside world is still very much getting to grips with supressing cruel prejudice and ignorance towards gay people and gender identity. We come from a very binary, black and white view of the

surveillance, lack of worldly education, not being able to follow your dreams, shame, fear and shunning. These are just some of the things we were constantly exposed to as JWs members. This upbringing left me and many others with very deep scars and issues, which in my personal opinion (I know that others may not agree) cannot be successfully overcome or healed without professional help.

When you are ready, move on. Please reach out to others who are in a similar situation, make friends with people outside of the organisation, talk and share. Immediately after you leave, joining cult survivor communities can be helpful. It personally was for me, although I now find that I no longer want or most days need the support of these [ex-Jehovah's Witnesses] groups. However, I've made some amazing friends there and they helped me through very difficult times.

I would also like to say that you will go through a grieving process after leaving the organisation. Allow yourself that grace, be patient and kind to yourself, but please make sure that you don't stay in that angry bitter place for too long.

We've given enough of our time serving this organisation and not living our lives as our true selves.
The best way now is to live your life to the fullest and leave the past in the past."

to throw everything in that they don't agree with. So, anything other than heterosexual sex for the purposes of procreation is thrown into the same sin pot. This way they can mix some natural sexualities into the same cauldron of evil as child molestation, rape and spousal violence. That isn't just ridiculous, its highly offensive and very dangerous. People's lives have been devastated by Elders expelling and publicly humiliating gay and bisexual Jehovah's Witnesses, and yes, they are many, just like there is in any natural society.

What is even more disturbing is the fact that when it comes to disciplinaries and public knowledge of so-called offences committed in the congregation, child abuse, rape and spousal violence are kept secret and quiet away from the congregation so as not to bring public reproach to Jehovah. Yet, those offenses that sit alongside such as homosexuality and gender fluidity are publicly victimised in front of the congregation. So, in actual fact, they aren't really treated the same way at all.

world and the world isn't like that, it's very colourful, brimming with variety and texture. The Jehovah's Witnesses want to make life simple and "ordinary" to the ridiculous point of telling you how long you should have your hair, what clothes you should and shouldn't wear, even having issues with having a beard. The Jehovah's Witnesses are stuck in a weird Nuclear Age, Fifties Americana. From the outside looking in it is very bizarre. Its ok if you are happy to fit into those little stereotypes of a yesteryear, but for anyone else it's a constant battle of wits against the Elders. That "simple life" is comforting to many devout Jehovah's Witnesses. But like the American Fifties culture and the once Victorian culture in the British Empire, it hides a very seedy and darker underbelly. The Jehovah's Witnesses organisation uses that darker underbelly

Many good people are forced away from their families and friends, humiliated and rejected. Many young people commit suicide because of this treatment. It is a pandemic caused by a controlling and manipulating religion.

With both sexuality and gender, there is a very wide and colourful variety of natural ways to be a human being that is only recently starting to be recognised and appreciated. I remember when I was very young, that when it came to race, most people in the community knew only white and coloured. That was the backwards binary way of thinking and the way most people saw the world without meaning to be mean. But now we know how offensive the word "coloured" is. Because there isn't just white and non-white people, there is a full spectrum of culture and a world of different peoples, cultures and races, not just the western white population. It is offensive because it is ignorant.

And that can also be said about sexuality and gender. There isn't only "straight" and "Nun". There are all sorts of colourful types of gender and sexuality that range throughout the human condition. To ignore those extra colours, will likely show one's ignorance and a lack of compassion. It's natural to feel overwhelmed with it all, to feel lost and embarrassed. But it only takes a little research on the internet to get to grips with it all. It's worth it in the end to find out about these kinds of things because, just like we tried to do in the organisation, all we really want to do is be good to people and be compassionate. Only now, once outside of the organisation, we can do it in an educated way and without prejudice.

You may also find yourself challenged by other religious viewpoints and what you may think as unorthodox faiths, even pagan faiths. Just remember to be tolerant. If people wish to do good in their lives, then that has to be better for everyone, as long as bigotry, hatred and violence are not part of a person's faith, then really, we should give them some respect. Just because someone else's reality is not a carbon copy of your own, there is no need for tribalism and intolerance.

You might find that you jump to conclusions about other people's faith. There are too many people in the western world that seem to believe that all Muslims are hateful terrorists and you might find your current belief moves that way, having picked up heavy prejudice from the congregation. It doesn't take much to realise that most religious faiths are mostly made up of good people trying to be kind and loving to their fellow human beings.

It is our uneducated prejudice that makes us jump to conclusions about the outside world. Paganism and witchcraft are a typical example of this. From the standpoint of a Jehovah's Witnesses, we see these beliefs as wrapped in satanism, worship of the devil, bloodletting, curses, raising demons, dancing naked around fires, killing and torturing and exonerating evil. This is such an old Hollywood version of Paganism and witchcraft. It is quite an eye opener to talk to someone that follows this form of faith as those stereotypes are so far from reality that it's insane. They are all loving, caring heavily spiritual people that worship the earth and the body as a universal whole. Look after yourself, all life around you and the planet you live in. That is the basis of the pagan faith which couldn't be further from the picture we bring out of the Jehovah's Witnesses organisation with us.

Finally, politics. As Jehovah's Witnesses we had the luxury of keeping out of politics. You are not obliged to have a political opinion in the outside world. Please, though, remember to be respectful of other people's political views. If you wish, discuss them with others and do have an opinion if you desire, that is the beauty of free thinking. Remember that if you do decide to have a political opinion, if you do start to say what you think about the Councils, the parties, the Government, the Police or anything to do with the political system at all, then unless you vote, you will be seen as a hypocrite. Having a political opinion and not voting is like the Jehovah's Witnesses declaring truths about the outside world that they have nothing to do with. Even if you believe that voting is rigged and your vote means nothing, if you do not contribute by at least trying to vote, which costs you nothing at all except your right if not used, then you cannot truly express an opinion. It is fine to not be any part of the world, if you still choose to be, but that is very difficult to do when you live in a society where people have fought and died to give you the opportunity to mould the civilisation around you.

As with everything else, tolerance is required when listening to or expressing political opinion. Your opinion is as valid as anyone else's. Just make sure that violence, anger, hatred and fear don't cloud your politics and be aware of anyone else's politics that might be motivated that way.

"THERE IS LIFE AFTER THE JEHOVAH'S WITNESSES….

Many years ago, when our first daughter was born, my wife who was a devout JW refused the 'Anti-D Injection', as it was made from donated blood plasma. So consequently, when my second daughter was born, she was born terribly jaundiced. The hospital ward sister called me into her office and said they were going to put her under a special type of lamp to treat it, but if that didn't work, because her jaundice was so serious, there was a possibility that they would need to change her blood, and would I be prepared to give my permission. I said yes without any hesitation, but I asked her to please keep quiet about our conversation unless it became absolutely necessary, because I was a Jehovah's Witness; to which she agreed.

Fortunately, my daughter responded well to the lamp treatment, so the blood change wasn't necessary. If they [had] changed her blood, I think I may have been disfellowshipped from the JW's on the spot for allowing it; which wouldn't have done much for my relationship with her devout JW mother to say the very least. But it was a massive wake up call, as I realised I didn't and couldn't live by the JW rules for the rest of my life. So, I was living on borrowed time from then, and treading water as far as the religion and I were concerned. And sadly, I knew there really was no long term future with my wife, as she was a devout JW, and I was living a lie (I was actually a Ministerial Servant).
I think the final straw for me was when my JW father, who was an elder, ended up getting disfellowshipped for running off with another woman, after 28 years of marriage to my devout Witness mother. So that left me a bit confused after a very strict upbringing in the religion from birth to say the least. My father, even though he was an elder, used to knock me about all the time when I was a kid. I remember once when I was 14 he got me up against a wall and punched me in the stomach. When my mother told him to stop, he quoted the Bible Proverb "Spare the rod and spoil the child" to her.

I had played for time long enough for the sake of the children, and it had worked well; and I tried to play for even more time as my two children were still so young, but it didn't work. I couldn't keep up the pretence any longer, I really had had enough, so I finally resigned from the JW's.
Because of my resignation from the cult, I was shunned (I knew of course it would happen), and I lost a mother, a sister and virtually every friend I had overnight. A lot stay in it all their lives living a lie, rather than go through that, some even to the point of dying because they've refused a blood transfusion; I have been told that some decide to commit suicide because of the shunning.
One of the saddest days in my life was the time I was taking my 6-year-old daughter to Infants school, and she was crying in the back of the car. I asked her why she was crying, and she said, "I don't want you to die". A Jehovah's Witness had told her that I was going to die at Armageddon, because I no longer went to the meetings. She was 6 years old! That was 37 years ago, but it still makes me so angry when I think about it; but it makes me realise I made the right decision leaving the JW cult.

I have had a fantastic normal life since leaving the Jehovah's Witnesses. I have made a lot of new friends, genuine friends, not friends that shun you because you don't want to go to JW meetings or door knocking anymore. The best thing is, that because I left the cult, my 2 children realised that it was actually possible to leave the cult and live normal happy lives; and thank God they did. I hope this helps others make the right decision."

Anonymous

Beliefs

It is difficult when you lose everything, to then think about the good things you have inherited. The opportunity to now choose what you want to do with your life is an amazing gift that comes out of great sadness and sacrifice.

You are free to believe what you want. It is perfectly understandable that many choose to stop believing in anything at all to do with religion. You have been spiritually abused. You have been told that there is only one god and one faith and there will be many reasons that the Jehovah's Witnesses will have shaken your beliefs to the core.

Spirituality is a personal relationship between you and the universe around you. Because its personal to you, no one else can tell you whether that relationship is right or wrong, so long as it doesn't inflict damage on others either mentally or physically. Others may try and persuade you that their faith system is the only right one for you because either they need to bolster their own faith by persuading others of their beliefs or through a genuine concern that you might be being manipulated as you may well be vulnerable and under a crisis of faith.

You will get opinions from all sides. Other former Jehovah's Witnesses will be so sure of their own journey to reject all religions and become atheist that they may almost bully you into their way of thinking. Even atheists have a faith system. Faith is not only based on religion. We all have to have faith in peers, otherwise it we couldn't possibly grow as human beings. Imagine if we had to properly fact check absolutely everything people say to us or teach us. We would never have time to grow beyond some very basic understandings. People will try to convince you that because they don't have religion that they don't require faith. We all take things on faith. Most people will accept and believe in molecules, but very few have ever seen a photo of one and only a handful of people around the world have taken those photos. Yet we all believe molecules exist, we have faith that they exist.

If reality is just a personal interpretation of limited inputs and a singular experience, then how can anyone tell you what to have faith in. Just be aware of manipulation by others around you and those that harm others, especially through extremism. The Jehovah's Witness religion is an extremist religion. You have been entangled in an extremely strict and controlling regime with harsh and drastic consequences if you question or leave it. Although there is no doubt that the majority of Jehovah's Witnesses have good and honest intentions, it is stricken with many examples of extreme behaviour.

The core belief is that all non-Jehovah's Witnesses are going to be slaughtered in their billions when Armageddon is supposed to arrive. All Jehovah's Witnesses look forward to this with relish and cannot wait to get into a post Armageddon, paid for by the lives of 7 billion innocent people. They believe that all people outside the organisation are lesser human beings and deserve death when that time arrives. It is an unfortunate fact that the organisation covers up thousands of internal cases of child abuse worldwide. It is only after being outside of the influence of Jehovah's Witnesses that one can look back and see how extreme the controlling and oppression is amongst its members.

It is no wonder that when you leave, it is too easy to go headlong into another extremist belief or philosophy. At an ex-Jehovah's Witness person's core is that black and white, binary polarity that can be so easy to go and apply to many other beliefs or ways of life. It is a hard habit to break along the way and recognising those traits within yourself is the first step to truly being free.

To add to all these struggles is the natural desire to fit in. We all want to be accepted into a tribe and truly belong somewhere. It is human nature. There is comfort and safety to be found in belonging. Being rejected from somewhere you belonged is a massive blow to your personality and self. Once you leave or get expelled it is natural to go out and find another tribe to fit into. After the trauma of being a Jehovah's Witness, you might desire to no longer be seen as weird and different. Most people brought up strictly as Jehovah's Witnesses look back on a life of bullying, taunting and ridicule starting from being an infant at school through to being socially separated and awkward at work. It is likely that you have struggled your whole life to try and be "normal" and fit in, but as a Jehovah's Witnesses, no matter how hard you try, you always look and behave like an outsider. Many Witnesses spend their lives juggling their personalities between that which the organisation demands and following the desire to just be seen as "normal" by outsiders. Being aware of this deep seated desire will help you see how those desires will try and manipulate your actions and not always for the best. It is great to fit in somewhere, but be aware of where you want to fit in and why. After leaving the organisation, you will have undergone a great blow to your personality. You may not really know what you want from life or what you want to do going forward. Making rash decisions and throwing yourself headlong into another tribe, group, religion or society, might lead you to regret joining a group with the wrong ideals or you may see yourself compromising the moral ideals you thought you wanted to keep.

I was very fortunate to have learned a lesson about the desire to fit in years before I left the Jehovah's Witnesses. I was around 15 years old. I had two years of school left to go. My entire school years had been spent dodging one fight and another simply because I was so weird and stuck out like a sore thumb. I was the "Jovo" kid. Poor, shabbily clothed, very geeky and totally devoid of any other personality than that of being a Jehovah's Witness. I was trying to be a good Witness. I was being pressured to get baptised. I had duties at the Kingdom Hall which my mother was proud of. I had to walk six miles to the Kingdom Hall and back twice a week, along streets where my school colleagues lived. I did the preaching work around the houses of the school catchment area. I had to wear seventies hand-me-down suits from my uncle in the middle of the eighties. Everything about me was screaming out loud to get beaten up and the boys at school were always happy to answer that call. Every time I went home with bruises, my mother would punish me for getting into fights. I was totally afraid to ever retaliate in a fight, because if there was a thousand to one chance that a lucky punch could damage someone, I would be cast out from the congregation, I would be spiritually dead. So I resigned myself to get beaten.

This made my every fibre and my every desire to just be normal, to just fit in, be grey and invisible. I got into football just to be normal, I listened to pop music to be normal, I stopped wearing my geek spectacles at school and walked around half blind just to try and be normal. Yet even after years of trying to simply fit in, I was still so obviously different from anyone else.

It was under this stress that I confided in my grandfather. Strangely in our family, he was the only non-Jehovah's Witness and yet he would never have any word said against the principles and practices of the Witnesses when around him. He gave me advice about strength and being different.

My grandfather was born with a deformity in his left arm. It was twisted behind his back while in the womb. As he aged his arm remained smaller, shrivelled, purple and unusable. I grew up with his deformity, so I was totally used to it. He never let it hold him back in any way whatsoever. In fact, it gave him an edge, a proud stubbornness that nothing was going to get in his way as regards looking after himself. He worked his entire life at a steel tubing factory and was a well-respected and hard worker.

It used to shock me when the two of us were out in public and I would catch people staring at him. He always said that it was a natural reaction to be curious and to look, but some people would stop in the street and just stare at him as he walked past them, mouth hung open. I realised how ignorant and rude people could be. But he never let that get to him or stop him from doing anything. He always used to go swimming with us to the public baths and people would nearly drown staring at him. It was so rude. But to watch him tie his shoelaces one handed in a swift and practiced discipline was an amazing thing to see.

When I told my grandfather about the bullying and my constant embarrassment about being different, I knew he understood what being different meant. He told me to be proud to be different, to forge one's own path, to never be ashamed of who you are and, in fact, revel in your uniqueness instead of joining the

treadmill of popularity. Stand up proud and be your unique self and don't play to other people's rules and don't let others dictate to you how you should live your life in any aspect of it.

That advice eventually backfired on him. As I took on that advice and grew in confidence and showed more independence, the more he started to then tell me the opposite, that being different and being weird brought negative attention to the family and to myself. It was typical of the contradiction of the witnesses of which he was defending. I then started to get into trouble in the congregation for being different and not fitting into the strict personality of what the congregation regarded as normal.

It was then that I started to see how ridiculous some of things that we had been taught by the organisation was. We were told to "be no part of this world" and yet we were expected to be normal in the world. A man can't have long hair, or wear women's clothes. The acceptable types of clothes are only the ones the world will accept as "professional" and "gender specific". It's the world outside that has decided what those parameters are. The Governing Body hasn't made a clothing line that looks nothing like what everyone in the outside world wears. They have adopted an acceptable version of clothes that are acceptable to the outside world. That attitude isn't "no part of this world". This is how contradictory the whole of the Jehovah's Witness society is.

My being different and proudly being myself, almost stopped the bullying. No-one at school understood what I was anymore, so they mostly left me alone. As I grew older, I became more unique and individual without any shame. I was proud to be me, even though I still struggled with my personality due to losing the universe around me in the form of the Jehovah's Witnesses and then another blow later in life after a failed, long term relationship.

Being different has sometimes got me noticed in a negative way, but how can I be shameful of simply being myself. It has been a lifesaver to be able to stop pursuing the never-ending need to fit in. It has been one thing I haven't had to concern myself with or worry about, in fact it has given me the much-needed confidence and pride that I would never have had otherwise.

Thank you Grandfather, kind of.

Methods Of Leaving (or not)

How or whether you leave the Jehovah's Witnesses organisation is a choice you can only make. Don't let others dictate to you how you should leave or if you should leave at all. Only you know your heart and circumstances and know what you can live with and what is best for your own mental health.

I'll explain a few ways that people have chosen to either leave or hang on in there. I'll try and explain the pros and cons of each decision and why someone might choose that method. There is no right or wrong way, there is only what is best for you and those around you.

Stay in and submerse yourself.

You may decide that the risk of losing everything, including friends, family, community and your faith is just too much to cope with. This is your life and leaving the witnesses is no small decision and don't let anyone else convince you otherwise.

In the short term it may seem like it really is what you want to do. There may be many reasons you might have questioned or left, and they may not be reason enough for you to stay out of the congregation. You may well think that having glimpsed the outside world that the Jehovah's Witness organisation is where you really want to be. That, of course, is your choice. Please remember that it is not the whole world that will ignore you if you return to being a Jehovah's Witness, it is the Jehovah's Witnesses, your friends and family, that will make you an outsider if you leave. The Witnesses are the oppressors.

Returning to the congregation is not as easy as you may think. If you have been disfellowshipped or disassociated, you will likely have to go through the humiliating period of going to meetings, being publicly ignored, stared at and isolated in shame. You might think you know how long that period will be until the Elders see you are repentant and they re-instate you. For me, it was a few months, and it was hell. For others who I have spoken to, it has been a year or more and some wait for what seems like an eternity.

Then when you do get back in, you will never get back your former glory. You will always be damaged goods, the one with a blemish against them. You will always be marked. It turns any progress back in to feeling like a fully devoted and good witness, even more difficult than it was before. As a man you may find that it takes lots more work to attain responsibilities as you will always be looked upon with suspicion. It is not an easy path to return.

It is so difficult to try and put the genie back in the bottle. There is every possibility, that either on you journey out of the congregation or while actually out altogether, that you will have seen or heard things that put a chink in your faith or in how you see the Elders, the congregation or even the organisation itself. You may well find that you go back into the congregation with your eyes more open than before and notice a lot more hypocrisy and lies than you ever did before. That then puts you in danger of expressing yourself publicly or sharing a different opinion that could well get you into even more trouble than before without even realising it. That different viewpoint could also stop you following the "truth" with your whole heart as you may have done before. It is worth thinking about these things before you throw yourself back in again.

Why is that a problem, you may ask? Because in a way you potentially throw yourself back into a life threating situation. You need to make sure you truly want to follow that course, because you will have to give up your right to a blood transfusion if you were ever in need of it. You may end up giving yourself even more trauma and mental

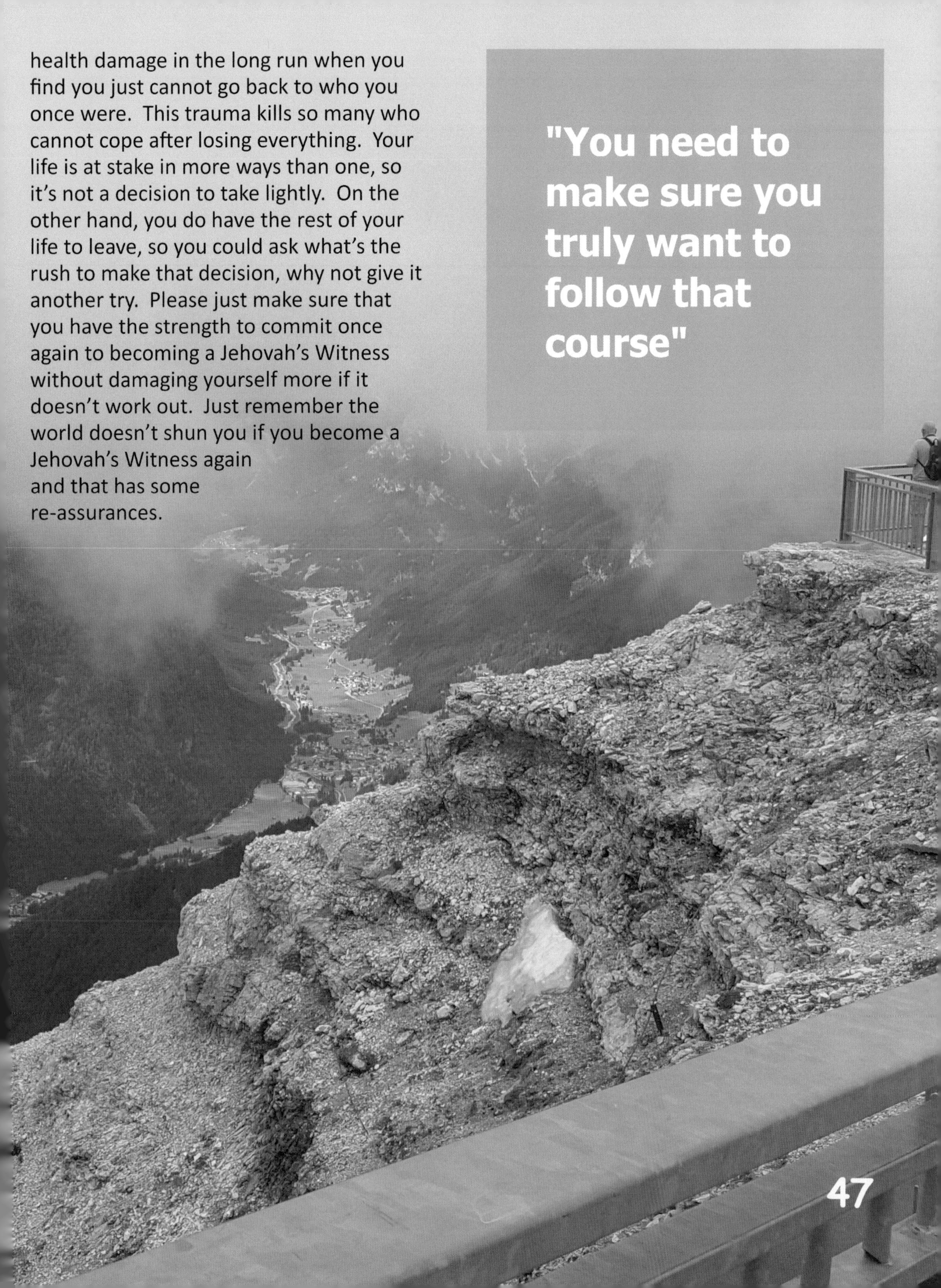

health damage in the long run when you find you just cannot go back to who you once were. This trauma kills so many who cannot cope after losing everything. Your life is at stake in more ways than one, so it's not a decision to take lightly. On the other hand, you do have the rest of your life to leave, so you could ask what's the rush to make that decision, why not give it another try. Please just make sure that you have the strength to commit once again to becoming a Jehovah's Witness without damaging yourself more if it doesn't work out. Just remember the world doesn't shun you if you become a Jehovah's Witness again and that has some re-assurances.

"You need to make sure you truly want to follow that course"

Stay in PIMO (Physically In Mentally Out)

It is estimated that a huge portion of Witnesses in every congregation are actually PIMO. Good people who have seen too much, witnessed things that have shook their faith to pieces, couldn't help but read some startling truths about the organisation or just become frustrated with a promise that never materialised while they missed out on so much of life and family.

It must be one of the most difficult positions to be in. Every ex-Jehovah's Witness deeply feels for anyone stuck in this position. You may have had enough, witnessed too much or just lost faith. In any other walk of life or situation, it would make perfect sense to just walk away. But of course, when you have your whole life wrapped up in being a Jehovah's Witness, it makes this a very difficult and seemingly impossible decision to make.

Leaving could well mean the loss of your family, all your friends, your community and the security you may have had around you for possibly decades if not your whole life. You may also think that you know so little of the world outside that sometimes it's a case of "better the devil you know".

But staying is a very hard and difficult life to lead. Before, you had a stronger faith and a complete belief system and it was difficult even then. Being a Jehovah's Witness is not an easy life by any means. It takes a lot of work, a lot of study, takes up all your time and leaves little time for family and being social. Even as a believer, most people feel like they are never good enough, always falling short, always failing to reach that pinnacle to strive for perfection even though you know you aren't perfect. When your faith and belief is shaken, this becomes an even harder task and if you really don't believe any of it at all, it becomes almost impossible. It will be as though you are just waiting for that one slip up, that one moment when the vail of smiles falters just that once and you get caught out.

You will need to bite your tongue, don't express any opinion, don't rock the boat and somehow live a double life where even your own family members could betray you at any time to the elders.

It is not a remotely enviable position to be in.

And yet, on the other hand, you will be with your family and friends, at least for a time. You will still be surrounded by the familiar. At least you know the rules, mostly. You will also unconsciously sow seeds of doubt in others. It is almost inevitable. People around you, those that know you best, will sense something is different and at some point, the veil will slip and that occasional influence could help others to begin to see the real truth about the organisation. That can only happen from within, that can only happen if you are there. You might also find out that the people you fear might shun you are actually going through the same mental anguish as you are. It has happened more than once, where huge numbers of Jehovah's Witnesses in one congregation have all left together, even to the point where a congregation has disbanded because of it.

The longer you live that life the harder it will get to cover your tracks. The Jehovah's

Witnesses organisation is very aware of their PIMO problem. After COVID, they have been struggling to get members to physically return to the Kingdom Halls. There is such a clear decline in physical numbers at Kingdom Halls and conventions that the organisation is desperate to get back to some form of normality. So there is added pressure to not only show yourself at the Kingdom Hall but also to be seen to be fully contributing in all aspects of being a Witness as the organisation gets more desperate to prove that numbers are not declining.

Only you can decide if this way suits your circumstances. Make sure you are ready for it though as it one of the toughest rides out of all these choices. Sometimes leaving can bring your loved ones with you.

One thing to remember is that the power of shunning only truly works and is effective when the majority of your family and friends stay in. Once there are as many people outside the organisation as in, the balance of that threat dissipates. Imagine that your family member is the only one left still stuck in the "truth" and everyone else has left. If that last family member decides to shun all their family, the only person they really punish is themselves. The more family members that are outside the organisation, the greater the pull is from outside for the rest still stuck inside and the shunning power has been diminished. You never know, you might be the catalyst that changes the balance amongst your family.

"I would advise most importantly to keep quiet. Don't confide in anyone that's still 'in', don't open your heart to them. Like it or not, the Elders still have power over you and could [disfellowship] you easily. Best avoided at all costs. BUT you still need someone to talk to and to listen to you, so make use of the ever-growing ex-[Jehovah's Witnesses] community. If you still pray, ask that you be put in touch with the right person to discuss things with, otherwise a conversation could just be a slag fest - not helpful to anyone.

Secondly, I'd say research, research, research. Not only the [Jehovah's Witnesses] teachings, but Christianity, other religions. Learn how the [Jehovah's Witnesses] fit in (or not), what position they hold. You'll soon see they are no different to any other religion, but you have to find this out for yourself.

Thirdly, look after yourself. Leaving the [Jehovah's Witnesses] is a major life change and can affect someone in all sorts of ways. So, eat properly, exercise, feed your mind on positive things and make new friends who share your doubts and find strength in each other."

Rosie Elliot - Author

Just fade

One of the more popular methods of leaving is to try and slip away quietly and hope the elders don't notice or care enough to bother you with dismissal. This has to be one of the least confrontational methods to get out. This method has been made easier post Covid when physical attendance at a Kingdom Hall was replaced with Zoom and online meetings. There is such a lack of transparency as to who is actually attending that many people could be slipping through the net and not be noticed. That is probably another reason why there is such a drive to get people physically back into the Kingdom Halls so that the organisation can physically work out more accurately the impact that Covid has had on the rapid decline in attendance.

Fading is where you slowly start to reduce the number of appearances at Kingdom Hall meetings or out on the carts or preaching work. This can very much depend on your profile as a Witness in the congregation. If you were a regular pioneer or an Elder that is always involved in every aspect of everyone's lives in the congregation, it's a lot harder to just disappear and the fade would have to be undertaken over a longer period of time so as to cause the least amount of suspicion and confrontation.

The problems you will face with a longer fade, is holding back on your newfound freedoms. There is such a relief when both your conscious and subconscious realise that you are not bound and forced to go to meetings. It may only take a few missing meetings, and once the initial guilt subsides and the habit begins to break, you may find yourself beginning to become extremely impatient and just wanting to stop altogether. Just be aware that it is likely to happen at some point and probably more prematurely than you planned. Remember as well, that for years, even decades in some cases, you will have had this habit-forming timeline of your week. You may feel awkward, as though you have an itch you cannot get to scratch. This is because a solid pattern has been formed in your life and breaking that pattern, while it can be euphoric, can also cause some strange withdrawal symptoms.

You may find that you miss your social circles. You may have been at the centre of social gatherings or all sorts of friendly dinners etc, but now you don't see people as often or happen to hear about something happening because you don't see people at the meetings, you become stuck outside of that social loop. That can impact you more than you think it will, especially when you realise that many people just get on with their lives without you.

Depending on how close your friends are to you, at some point someone will notice. Friends will ask where you have been and begin asking questions about what is happening with you. Everyone in this scenario has a temptation to confide in their close friends. But please remember, although they are your friends, no matter how close you think you are, their priority is to Jehovah. They will be sure in themselves that any deviation from the faith that you show can only be saved by immediately going and telling the elders. Remember how you used to feel. Your friends will think that they are saving your life but in reality they will be betraying you and your trust. I have talked to so many people that have had this done to them and it's hard not to take it very personally and feel very let down and deeply betrayed. Remember, they will do this out of love. They will have no concept of what it is they are doing to you when this happens. Be prepared for it as it catches so many fading witnesses out. If you are unsure, wait and let your friend show that they are questioning or doubting the faith before you confide in them and even then, still be wary. All manner of deceit seems justified if you think you are saving a loved one.

SCAN ME
SCAN ME

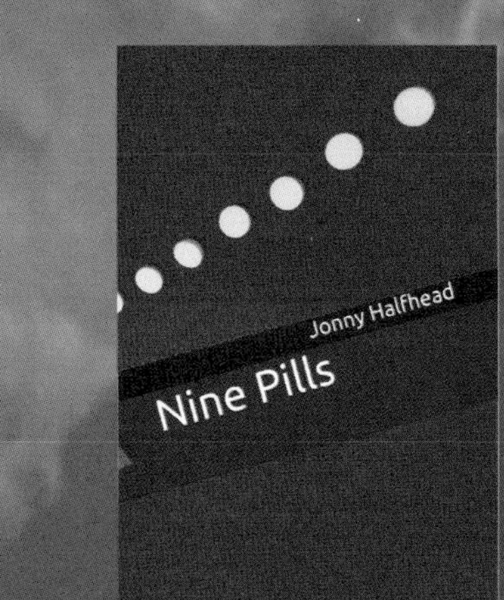

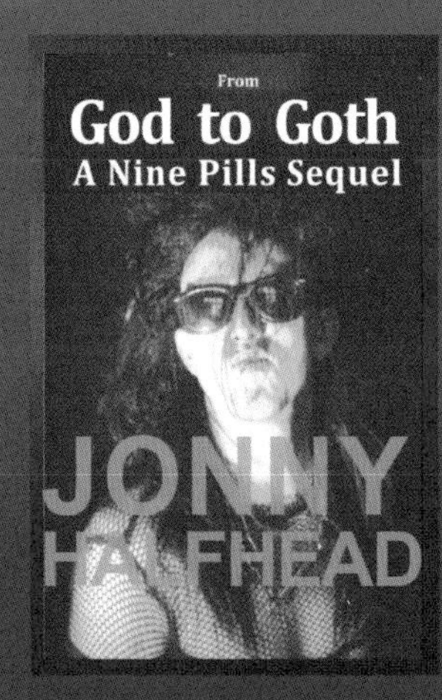

THE 1975
APOCALYPSE
JONNY HALFHEAD

The Offence
of Grace
JONNY HALFHEAD

The Books That Millions Of People Worldwide Are Banned From Reading

At some point you may find Elders begin harassing you and following you. In some congregations Elders feel the need to try and catch you out, to see you doing something worthy of disfellowshipping. Just as you may think that fading is a clever win-win scenario, Elders want to make sure you are expelled completely in order to give you up as an example to the congregation. They will also want to harshly treat you with their "tough love" and use disfellowshipping as a tool to try and shock you back into the congregation. I have seen plenty of examples of people trying to fade and having to call the police because of the level of harassment from Elders. You may find that they follow you, stalk you, sit outside your house and watch you. That is how far it can sometimes go.

If you are in a situation where you are fading and your marriage partner is still a full PIMI, this becomes especially difficult. If you are still close, your partner will quickly go to the Elders and try and get them to see you, counsel you and try and save you. It's just about impossible to fade while still married and living with a PIMI partner, you would have to remain squeaky clean in every aspect of your life and you just wouldn't benefit from any of the freedoms of leaving the Jehovah's Witnesses. That is not an enviable position to be in at all. Counselling would have to be an absolute priority for you just to keep your life and mental health together.

If you feel like you are splitting apart from your partner, just remember the position you will likely be leaving them in. You will have freedom to get on with your life, whereas a partner still stuck in the congregation, would never be able to move on with their lives without clear proof of you committing adultery. The only way a Jehovah's Witness can nullify a marriage is through death or adultery, so they will have a deep fear of being trapped unless they can try and trap you or catch you out. In this scenario, don't be surprised if a partner starts following you everywhere, tries to look at all your personal correspondence, anything that they can use to then free themselves of being trapped without hope of moving on. This can get a bit weird sometimes as they can follow you everywhere, desperate to find anything they can take to the elders.

As you begin fading, you may have to lie. That might seem obvious, as so much of our lives have been recorded. How many hours we did, what literature we bought to pass on, how much we donate, even down to whether we went to a Kingdom Hall while on holiday. Elders take an interest in a lot of these things.

It might seem obvious to lie about these activities, but so many of us just aren't prepared for it and aren't very good at doing it. It's been drilled into us that lying is one of the greatest of sins. Some people are just very natural at lying to the point that they even believe their own lies that they tell themselves. Many of us were convinced that god listens to our every thought and that everything we say is being remembered and recorded by god and he knows what is in our minds and hearts. To lie is to betray god and ourselves. I still personally believe that lying betrays our own persona, and that when we lie we lose a piece of ourselves. It would be difficult to fade without lying to some people, somewhere. This is your journey though, and you may feel that lying to people you loved and trusted is perfectly justified and that is your conscience call. Just be prepared for it and remember that you are likely not very good at it. Perhaps practice doing some little fibs first.

As with many of the methods of leaving, preparation is key. Be prepared within yourself for what may come and be sure it is what you want before you go on that journey.

Move to another congregation and then fade

There is a more clean-cut way of fading, which is probably the most successful as regards covering all the bases and that is by moving over to another congregation where no one knows you and then fade from there. This is not a simple solution if you cannot move home, or you live with a partner or family that still attend. But out of all the methods of leaving, this seems the solution that fares better overall.

It is not easy to do if you just decide to start going to a neighbouring congregation. For some reason Elders can get quite territorial about someone choosing of their own free will which congregation they wish to regularly attend. There are quite strict boundaries set out for each congregation catchment area and Elders can get very persuasive about whether they think you are doing wrong by regularly attending meetings somewhere else.

The further away geographically you are from your original congregation, the greater your chances of fading unnoticed. There is generally a sphere of influence in a congregation that radiates out into neighbouring congregations. Larger families can easily spread over to other geographically closer congregations and believe me that local gossip is always extremely rife across families.

If you have a Kingdom Hall that shares more than one congregation, you could use that other congregation to switch to in order to then fade from, but you may find that it has too many close links. The advantage with a Kingdom Hall that shares with more than one congregation is that you could use the convenience of the other congregations meeting times as a reason to move over. It's a sound reason. You could even keep switching between one and the other. That way, after a short while, everyone from each congregation will assume you are attending the other congregation that week, if that was a habit you had already taken time to build.

The further away the congregation is from the one you attend, the quicker you can phase your fade. Moving across the country means you could probably simply stop attending straight away, as no one would be any wiser.

#igotout

Freedom of thought is a universal human right.

Share Your Story.
Impact Lives.
Make a Difference.

Find out more at igotout.org

@igotout_org on the socials

Family are the ones more likely to be watching you and keeping a close eye on what you are doing. Many congregations can seem very incestual and close with lots of family ties across them. There are always eyes and ears everywhere feeding the rumour mill that never stops turning.

If you are reading this as a still fully devoted Jehovah's Witness, you will very likely snub these generalisations and say that the congregation is not like that at all. But just you see what it is like when you try and leave. It is, again, another sign of a cult, the way that organisation lets you change your mind and leave. Jehovah's Witnesses say officially that they do not stop anyone leaving, but they do watch, harass and punish those that exercise their right to choose. Once you try to leave, you will suddenly see a totally different side to the organisation, one that strangles and controls every aspect of your life.

Write a letter of Disassociation

This is when a person writes a letter addressed to either the Elders or to the congregation, which that person writes to make it clear they no longer wish to be a Jehovah's Witness anymore. A person can get to a point where they feel they want closure and a clean cut from their former life and the control that goes with it.

I have seen many people have a very sudden wake up. After years of being a devoted Jehovah's Witness something happens that suddenly triggers a totally different viewpoint. All at once the veil falls and the real truth starts to reveal itself. This shocking revelation has almost a cascading effect, where once you start looking and doing more and more research, the more things you find disturbing, disgusting and horrific. It's a natural reaction to find that you are disgusted in yourself for being duped and taken in by it all and also by the whole organisation for lying and deceiving you so obviously.

In that state of anger, it is no wonder that many people want to loudly counteract and publicly dismiss what they were once were a part of by creating a letter of disassociation. Because of that reaction, you may feel the need to shut yourself off from the organisation. You made a public display once by getting baptised and making a lifelong promise to serve. It is quite understandable that you may want to then make the same kind of statement

because that promise was made under duress or deception, that another public declaration is needed to counteract that original contract.

It may be wise to ask yourself why you would want to write and send this letter. In many ways it does make a lot of sense, to make a clear demarcation line, to stop a former life of oppression and deception and start again, clean and new. It might be that you want to fight back and show that you are no longer controlled and manipulated. You may want to tell the Elders or your former congregation some home truths about what you have found out and learned about the organisation.

You need to bear in mind, that only an Elder will see that letter and its highly likely that they will probably not even read all of it through. An Elder's role has made that person adept at separating out any language in the letter that might be seen as apostate or bitter while they read it. It is highly unlikely that any of the reasoning, or time and care put into a letter, will actually have any impact on anyone in the congregation at all. The only action it might incur is a brief announcement at a weekday meeting that you are no longer a Jehovah's Witness. If you have been gone some time and the congregation is unlikely to remember you, an announcement will likely not occur at all and the letter will just be filed away. Many ex-Jehovah's Witnesses do find comfort in writing a letter and it makes sense why. It does feel as though you can take some power back, that you have decided the time and place to be cut off and someone else hasn't done that to you. It feels like a direct response in the face of your oppressors and abusers.

Then again, it might not feel that way once you have done it. Imagine if you

had been conned on a holiday time share scheme and you found out you had been scammed and lost money to the scammers. You would rightfully be angry, annoyed, hurt and embarrassedby the scammers. But you wouldn't want to write a letter to the scammers explaining to them why you didn't want to be part of the scam anymore and that you refuse to send them anymore money. Sending a letter would almost be accepting that they are the people they said they were. It would hand back some power to the scammers because you still feel a part of the con story.

The same could be said about a letter of disassociation. It still acknowledges that the Elders have power over you, that they are more than just poorly educated set of self-appointed leaders. It implies that there is still a rule of law and a set of procedures to follow and comply with and be part of the organisations processes. It doesn't admit that you are fully free of its influence, quite the opposite in fact. In some ways, you still believe in the scam.

On the other hand, it can be a very worthwhile step to take if you feel you need to do it for the sake of your own healing. It may give you some closure and mark a clear line in the sand that says, "no more". That is all totally understandable and once again it is a personal choice for you on your own journey and isn't for anyone else to tell you what choices you should make. That is the beauty of freedom. Just be aware that even though it will be a line you have drawn, your inner self still needs to carry on healing. The trauma and the consequences on your mental health will not just go away at that one moment in time, you will still need to address your mental health even after that line has been drawn.

Get disfellowshipped

Most of the time this isn't really a chosen method of leaving, it's just something that happens after a person does something that generally doesn't warrant the type of punishment dealt out. Being disfellowshipped is humiliating and soul destroying and changes a person's life in one fell swoop.

Strange as it seems, some people have opted for this as their method of leaving. I suppose if you wanted to exit proudly, loudly and abruptly, this method would accomplish that. It's easy to get disfellowshipped. You can lie to the Elders and tell them you did something you didn't do. You could take up smoking in public, although that does have greater life consequences, obviously. You could go out and try and have sex with someone so that at least you could say you got disfellowshipped with honesty. Good luck with trying to accomplish that, it's not as easy out in the world as you might think to just have sex with someone. You could try and spread the word of freedom from the clutches of the organisation all around the congregation, that will definitely get you noticed and swiftly disfellowshipped and you might, at least, take someone with you by opening their eyes in the process.

This isn't the best way to exit. This is usually a reactionary process, fuelled by anger because of what you may have found out about your life with the Witnesses and while anger is understandable, maybe even justified to some level, it doesn't help the people you leave behind, still trapped inside the organisation. In fact, getting disfellowshipped in such a passive manner will no doubt fuel the propaganda machine that is hard at working keeping all those you know and love deeper in its controlling and manipulative grip.

Cut yourself off

This method might seem quite simple and straightforward. Just leave one day and never go back. Stop all access to family and friends yourself as you may see that being cut off by them is inevitable anyway, then at least the control is in your hands, you decided and wrote the narrative.

Unfortunately, this method rarely works. Occasionally people do get away with it. But most of the time, an abrupt stop makes people in the congregation sit up and take notice and not in a good way. For some reason the organisation and the Elders do not lot like you taking control at all. They will go to great lengths to find out what you are doing and then try to take control of the situation themselves. It is a battle of personal power over your ability to make your own decisions in a public forum. It would seem that most Elders don't want you to be an example of steering your own course in life.

So, the Elders will try and either nag you back into returning to the congregation, or get you to say something to them that would justify them disfellowshipping you. Or, they will just sit around and put you under surveillance and try and catch you smoking, or spending time with someone privately, anything that they can use to simply accuse you of sinning and then, once again, disfellowship you but this time without your input.

Now, you might say that this is ridiculous, that Elders don't do those kind of things as they have enough workload as it is. Unfortunately, I have heard this story so many times where Elders behave this way. It is as though the congregation feels the need to take control back away from you even after you try and leave. Most of the time this method ends up morphing into one of the other methods of leaving and rarely works out. People either go back into the congregation after being fed up with the harassment and then fade instead, or they get disfellowshipped, sometimes confessing to something they haven't done, just to get the Elders off their backs and some move congregations and fade. On many occasions a person has had to get the police involved to stop Elders from harassing them and to force Elders to leave them alone.

Just be wary that if you choose this method, it can get quite creepy and it takes a lot of personal strength of character to accomplish. An understanding and sympathetic family can always be a huge help when trying to leave this way and can be the main ingredient for success.

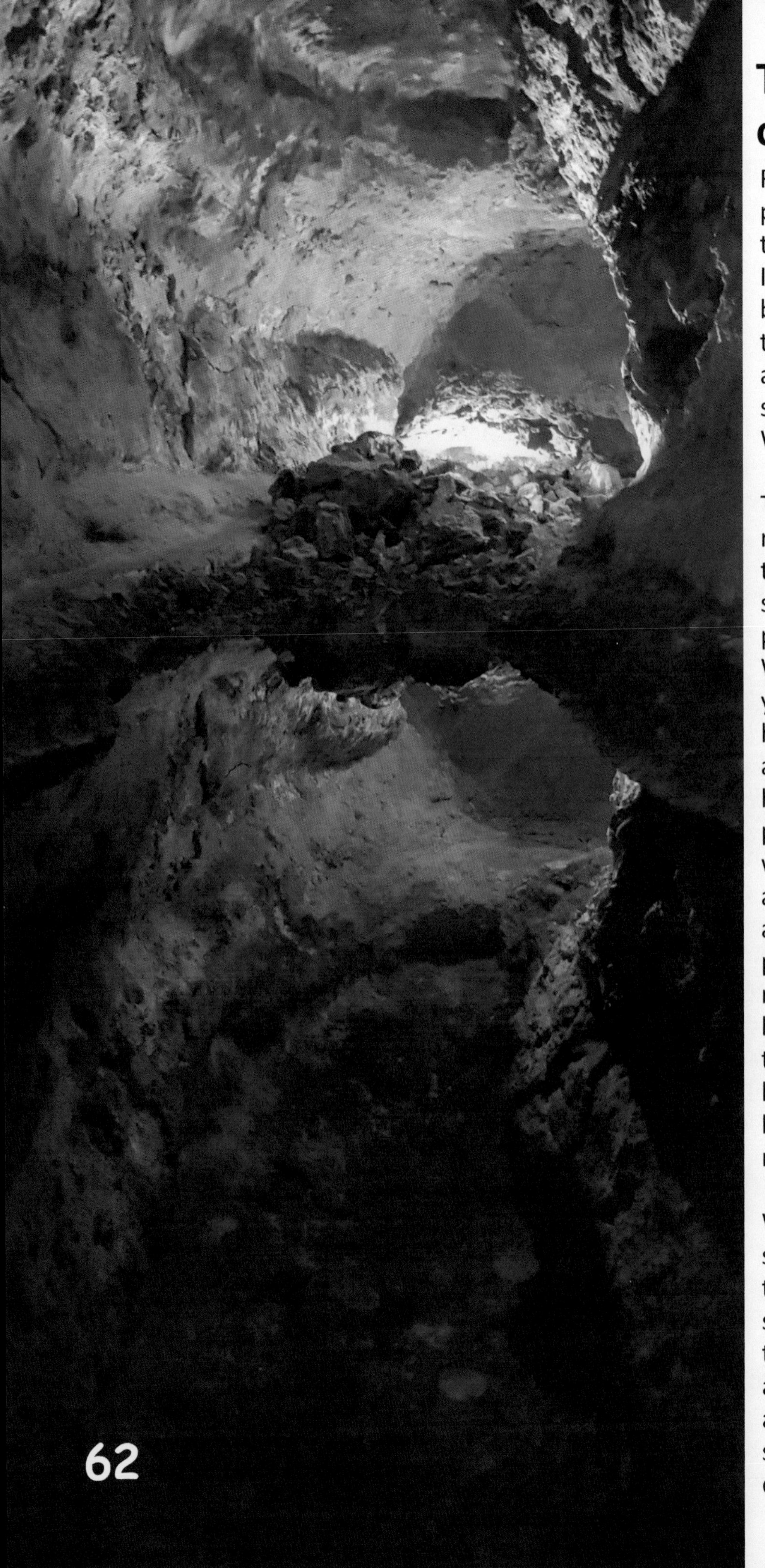

That most terrible of ways to leave

Finally, the one choice some people make which is the most tragic and the most terrifying. I don't really want spell it out, but I feel that to be honest and truthful, that I must. Suicide is a choice made too often after someone leaves the Jehovah's Witnesses organisation.

There may be a number of reasons why you may think that this is a solution to the seemingly insurmountable pain that you are feeling. Whatever the background of your pain is, however deep the hurt and loneliness may run, all I can say to you is that I have been there, at that same point, and decided that suicide was the only way out from it all. So how on earth do I go about convincing you that this place that you are in, is not a reflection on the rest of your life. I can only say to you that there is hope. Not just a little hope, but an entire universe of hope outside of where you are now.

When I tried to commit suicide, I didn't actually want that much from life, just a few simple things that I never thought was possible for me to attain. And yet, not only did I attain those goals, but have far surpassed them. I'm here, currently writing my sixth

"You don't have to be the person the JWs said you'd become. There are more good people in the world than there are bad. More people who want to help others and build on society than there are those who want to hurt others and destroy society. We know this because you hear more from the latter because it stands out as unusual.

It's OK to ask for help, and there is a whole community of people out there who want to help. You can be part of that community one day, if you want to. Love yourself and be kind to others. That's all you need to be a good person. You don't need a religion telling you what to do."

Terri O'Sullivan - Apostate Services Development Officer at FaithToFaithless

book, something I never would have thought possible.

Your mind probably reads this and thinks along the lines of "well that's alright for you". It is true that everyone's story is different and there are a lot of people that seem to just have things fall into place for them. But I had nothing at all when I left, as did a lot of people I have known that come out from the Jehovah's Witnesses and, yet, they have somehow managed to become some of the most amazing people I have ever met and have developed into the warmest and most loving individuals. I am here wondering how on earth I can convince you of what great things are before you and how your current view of the world around you and the effect it is having on you is heavily filtered.

If you are in that dark place, it is very hard to see any way out of it. The whole world seems isolated, cold and lonely. Your mental state imposes heavy filters and a restriction on your outlook and the image of how everything is around you. If it can be said that Jehovah's Witnesses are like a whole society of people stuck down the bottom of a wishing well and making assumptions on a world they cannot really see, your mental state will have become very similar.

Anxiety and depression are the worst of inflictions because they narrow your perception, force illness and sickness on you and make you believe that you at an end of all things. It is a horrible place to dwell. But here is light, there is hope and there is a different reality so close to you, if only you can allow yourself to see it. Don't underestimate the trauma you have suffered. It is not unremarkable, it is no little thing. Your suffering is real. You need to look for help and even though you may think that there is no help out in the outside world, there is so much that you will be surprised.

Reach out to other ex-Jehovah's Witnesses, people who have definitely been through similar situations to yours. The shadows that surround you now are not the monsters that you think they are. Seek professional therapy, specifically counsellors that deal with religious and cult trauma. Join closed JW support groups on social media where you will be safe and free to make friends and talk without congregational judgement.

Sources of Support

Faith to Faithless - faithtofaithless.com

Samaritans - samaritans.org

Family Survival trust - thefamilysurvivaltrust.org

Hope Valley Counselling - hopevalleycounselling.com

ExJw Counselling - exjwcounselling.co.uk

www.exjwsupport.co.uk

A few shocking truths

At the moment, you may think that the Jehovah's Witnesses are a worldwide, impossibly powerful entity that wields great influence over everyone it has ever touched. The reality could not be further from the "truth". In most of the outside world, Jehovah's Witnesses are barely known, in some parts not at all. We used to live inside a myth that gods organisation is so important that it is central to world affairs, that everyone in the outside world is being told, in detail, what is about to come and destroy them. That just isn't what is happening. Jehovah's Witnesses numbers are declining quite rapidly and so is the minimal influence they have around the world.

If you really talk to the everyday person outside the organisation, the vast, vast majority don't have a clue who Jehovah's Witnesses are, never mind what their message is. In the western world some people will have perhaps known someone, or had someone knock at their door once, but they will not have any idea at all as to what they actually are, what they stand for and what their message is. I've heard it said so many times outside the organisation that Jehovah's Witnesses aren't even Christian.

I have known former Jehovah's Witnesses that left the organisation decades ago, who still don't tell anyone that they used to be a Jehovah's Witness because they think that it carries some universal hatred and shame from everyone in the world. It's always a shock for a former Witness to realise that Jehovah's Witnesses are just insignificant in the local area, in the country, in the world.

Do you know about the Elders manual? Unless you were an Elder, you would never have known about the manual given to only Elders as a guide and containing instruction for how an Elder should perform his duty and what the precise rules are and when to keep the congregation in check and also how or when to discipline, etc.

This manual has been given to Elders with the very strict instruction not to allow anyone else but Elders to see it or know of its existence and definitely not to allow anyone but an Elder to read it. It even offers instruction on who can bind and cover the manual to keep it secret. Not even an Elder's wife is supposed to have knowledge of this document. The instruction is to keep it locked away so that even if an Elder's wife knew about it, she cannot be tempted to go and look at it. There are contents in that book that are not shared out with the rank and file Jehovah's Witness publisher. Each congregation member is being held accountable and punished by a set of rules they are not even allowed to openly study or read. As a Jehovah's Witness we always used to say that at least we belonged to an open, truthful and honest society, where the rules are clear, and the punishments known. Unfortunately, that just isn't the case. If you see your Elder, ask them how you are supposed to know what the rules are, if some of these rules are listed in a secretive and private book hidden inside the congregation itself.

You may ask why the Elders are supposed to keep this document and its contents secret. That is because it details the fine routes that some can take to find shortcuts out of getting punished for wrongdoing. For instance, if a certain amount of time has elapsed since a sin was committed and nothing was known about it, the sin can be dismissed. A baptism can also be annulled according to some rules stated in the book. There are clear guidelines of when a woman has officially been raped and when not. That alone would upset almost anyone reading it who would find it very disturbing. The same can be said about the rules surrounding the recognition of child abuse within the congregation. It is a fascinating and also deeply disturbing document that non-Elders are mostly not even aware of. How can a person who wishes to be pure and abide by the rules set out by the Jehovah's Witnesses organisation follow the rules when they aren't even allowed to see the publication that sets out those rules?

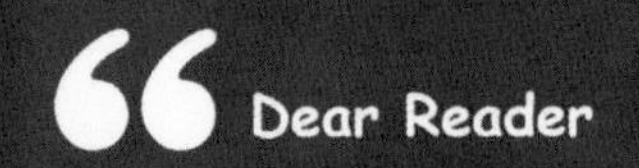

Dear Reader

I'm going to lay it on the line and be totally honest with you, leaving this faith is not easy. It will take a huge toll on your emotional and physical wellbeing. When you leave, you'll almost certainly lose your believing friends and family, in many cases, your entire social support system. If they follow you and wake up, you'll gain them back again far stronger and better than ever before, but that lonely, bleak time when everyone shuts you out will be the worst. Everyone you ever cared about will suddenly treat you as though they no longer care, under the guise of something which they have been brainwashed, or brow beaten, into believing is a "loving arrangement"

The general thought is that if you areshunned, cast out and sent to spiritual Coventry, then the sheer unbearableness of it all will force

you to repent and return. It's conditional love wrapped up in a blanket of unscriptural doctrine.

You'll have to pick apart the pieces of what's left of you, pore over every element of your former belief system, unravelling it until it is a messy, tangled pile of raw material, which you then have to sort through, piece back together in a shape and form which fits you comfortably, makes sense to you, reflects your style and values and above all, is something you can clothe yourself with to weather future storms.

Having now painted the picture very black and bleak, it's important to say this is the worst part, everything from hereon in gets better!

Yes, you'll have some dark days where all you want to do is cry and curl up under the covers, not have to go out and face the world outside. That big, scary, condemned "Worldly" World you were warned so fervently about. There will be days you'll question who you REALLY are? What do you really believe? What is your purpose in life now that your old path is behind you and your new one looms in front of you?

It's scary and daunting and can all feel like too much, especially if you've had a lifetime of being taught that there's only one place confidence is acceptable. You've been taught you must boldly go from door to door, proudly knock on each and every one, confidently speak to complete strangers about an emotive and often divisive subject. You were schooled from the cradle upwards that this was the only confidence you were ever allowed to exhibit.

To show too much faith in yourself, or

anything outside of your belief system, to think a little too much of your capabilities, or heaven forbid even say positive things about yourself instead of always others, was to show a wicked, selfish, independent spirit. You will have spent a lifetime of toning self-pride and appreciation down, squashing doubts, shelving questions on the never ending Jehovah shelf awaiting new light and cramming yourself awkwardly into a constrictive tick box, the four square walls surrounding you being ones made of rigid, outdated and excessive rules and laws designed to enclose your whole being and keep you stunted in every way possible.

The good news is though my friend, that you have made it through all of that, you've weathered all of that storm and made it to the other side, where you can now begin to truly ask questions and find proper answers, enjoy life the way it was meant to be enjoyed and really do anything you set your heart and mind to!

You are not alone in this, there are thousands of shining little beacons all across the world who will happily help guide you through this process, be a friendly ear, a comforting shoulder, a helpful word. People who have been where you are today, alongside people at the same stage of your journey who can travel the road ahead beside you. People united in one purpose, to truly care from a perspective of unconditional love and who want only one thing - your happiness. What works for one person might not for another, but I found there are a wealth of these people on ex JW internet forums, social network groups and video streaming channels. I found having a laugh about it all was the best sort of medicine. After I was done crying my tears of grief for the paradise I thought I would never see due to my sinfulness, I eventually realised I must make my own paradise, filling it with the things I love, the people I care about and the hopes and dreams I look forward to, not the ones enforced on me from childhood.

There is lots of help out there, it can be hard to take that first step but please, please reach out, make new connections, find your new people, start afresh. It's an honour to have been asked by Jonny to write this short piece and I hope it helps you in some small way.

My inbox is always open to anyone who wants to talk.

Yours with love

Helen Van Dahl

Most Jehovah's Witnesses believe quite strongly that to lie and deceive is a sin. In fact, it is at the heart of the belief system and that lying is at the root of evil. Satan is described as a liar and the great deceiver. It is one of the basic principles of Christianity and is at the core of a person's faith. And yet, almost in plain sight, and on more than one occasion over the past few decades, the Watchtower has told its followers that in some cases, lies are acceptable to god. I imagine that most Jehovah's Witnesses have barely registered or seen those instructions hidden in plain sight.

The Watchtower has said that if a greater good is being served then deception is acceptable. The wording is so cleverly done to the point that they strongly infer, without actually saying, that it is ok to lie if it saves the organisation's face or deflects negativity against the organisation. They are very clever in the way they use language to tell you without spelling out the words, even suggesting that Jesus himself deceived. You may think that this is impossible, but do your research in the organisation's own literature and you will wonder how you never noticed. Frighteningly, they say that under "Theocratic warfare" that this is acceptable, a turn of phrase that has been used repeatedly and only when you are no

longer a Jehovah's Witness do you realise how dangerous this type of propaganda is to its audience.

This attitude of the organisation telling versions of the truth has manifested itself in many examples that are well documented and seem almost impossible to believe, but are unfortunately very real. You can easily find proof of one of the governing body members lying while live on video to an Australian Court of Law, while under oath and having sworn on his own bible to tell the truth. It is footage from the Australian Royal Commission that investigated a pandemic of child abuse within religious organisations in Australia. It is footage that has to be seen to fully appreciate the magnitude of the lie and the deception.

Another example is the lies and deception about the Jehovah Witnesses organisation being paid members of the United Nations for a number of years at the beginning of this century. Any Jehovah's Witness would know that the United Nations is the beast from Revelations. It has false religion, Babylon the Great, riding that beast, signifying Christendom controlling the United Nations. The hatred of the United Nations has been a staple of the Jehovah's Witness doctrine for a hundred years. And yet, because it had political advantage to do so, the Jehovah's Witnesses organisation made itself paid members of the United Nations for a number of years.

Proof is very easy to come by. The United Nations has documentation you can download on its website. The United Nations put the documentation on its website because its administration was getting fed up with constantly being asked for proof from former Jehovah's Witnesses that couldn't believe this had happened. The organisation has made excuses several times to newspaper enquiries about the matter, stating that they just wanted access to the United Nations libraries and that they could only do so by being paid members. That is a weak excuse from an organisation that claims the United Nations to be despicable.

The Jehovah's Witness organisation has also been in trouble several times for mis-quoting science specialists and using expert opinion in a deceptive way. Some older publications have had to be edited or withdrawn because the specialists whose quotes were used have sued the Watchtower for misuse of their scientific papers.

According to Jehovah's Witnesses teachings, when god supposedly looked down on the earth for a religious group to represent him in 1919, he saw what was to become Jehovah's Witnesses and chose them from amongst all the world's religions. But they were not the organisation that you have been led to believe they were. In fact, you wouldn't recognise that religion until at least the 1950's as being anything like the Jehovah's Witnesses organisation that it is now. Racism in the organisation was rampant. The organisation had the same view as a lot of society did at the time, that people of colour were inferior. Some of the language used in publications and at convention speeches was downright evil.

This was further demonstrated by an open letter that Rutherford wrote to Hitler in the 1930's praising Hitler for his stance against Jews, a stance which Rutherford said the Jehovah's Witnesses shared. Rutherford also made other parallels with the beliefs of the Witnesses and the Nazi regime in Germany.

One of the hardest things to get your head around is the likelihood that you are not living in the worst time of human history ever known. It was drilled into us that these are the last days, a time that is without any doubt the most terrible and terrifying time that humankind has ever known. In the publications it is repeated to us over and over that war, famine, pestilence and earthquakes are all the actual signs that we are living in the time of the end. This was something I truly believed, something that couldn't be disputed.

When you take a while to just take a step back and look around, in so many ways those statements that just aren't true. If you wanted to live in any other time in human history, would you honestly pick any other time than now? Even a hundred years ago, before penicillin was discovered, you could die so easily from a scratch or a simple infection. Life expectancy has rocketed in the last hundred years. Even in the richest countries just a hundred years ago, you would have to have been born into great wealth to be assured food and shelter. In the west, we are very fortunate to have the life we are born into.

The Covid crisis was unprecedented in the fact that so many people went to so much trouble to save so many lives. The technology to save people's lives has become so ordinary, that we feel the need to have conspiracies against that which heals us so that we don't have to be grateful for what we have.

So many diseases and sicknesses that killed millions of people in the past have either been eradicated or controlled down to a minor threat. Although hunger and the amount of poverty in the world is still very prevalent, it hasn't been anything like the epic scales of just a hundred years ago. The world we live in today is unrecognisable even from half a century ago. I would not like to live in any other period in human history than the current one, as my chances of survival are magnitudes greater than they would be at any other period in history.

This is one of the reasons why the population growth has expanded at an unprecedented rate in the last 100 years. Survival is expected today.

The one "fact" that had me convinced of the truth, was the number of deaths by volcanoes and earthquakes that the Jehovah's Witnesses organisation says changed exponentially since 1914. I honestly believed that statement of fact from the organisation and, for me, it was hard proof that we are living in the last days. I thought those figures were undisputed. It wasn't until I was able to do some independent research and chatted to a few geological societies in America by email (it was the early days of the internet) that I found out that for the last hundred years we have been in a very quiet period as regards to the number of eruptions and tectonic movements. On top of that discovery, I also found that less people die now from such seismic activities simply because we build safer and have more accurate warnings and predictions. This is the absolute opposite of what we were all told by the organisation. Deaths from earthquakes and volcanoes have dramatically fallen in the last hundred years, not risen.

The biggest feather in the cap for Jehovah's Witnesses when it comes to foretelling the future is the prediction of war. There is no doubt that World War One was a global change in warfare that started in 1914. But that was not predicted by the Jehovah's Witness organisation in the way they constantly say it was. The founder of the religion, Charles Taze Russell, had made many predictions prior to 1914. That year was one of a long list of dates on which he predicted that things would happen and signified some spiritual fulfilment. He came across these dates using mathematical equations used from the structure of the great pyramids in Egypt, using specific points on the pyramids as date references for his predictions. Not one of the other dates prior to 1914 stood up to anything and they failed quite publicly. 1914 was the last date that Russell had predicted to be significant and it was to be the final date, the year of Armageddon, god's war on earth where all the wicked would be destroyed and paradise would begin.

As awful as World War One was, it wasn't the end of the world, it wasn't Armageddon. The scale of that war was unlike anything else seen before in terms of numbers, but then surely with the increase in world population, that is always going to be the case. World War Two then jumped another step up as you would expect with a larger population growth.

In terms of impact on the human race, neither of the two world wars have had the same impact as the Mongol Conquest of the 13th Century by Genghis Khan. Those wars killed an estimated 11 percent of the world's population of the time, next to the 3.3 percent that World War 2 inflicted on the human race. And isn't it interesting that the Mongol Empire is not included in the listed world empires of Nebuchadnezzar's dream, which goes from the Roman Empire straight to an imagined Anglo-American empire. Has there ever been an Anglo-American empire in the context of a ruling empire over the world. I think historians have quite a bit to say about this "fantasised simplification of history".

It is best for you to form your own opinions on such matters though. Do your own research. Try and find trustworthy sources with no other agenda. Scientific journals, historical societies, university papers, etc are probably a good source as they have to be challenged and reviewed when published. Take in what you can, apply some common sense and see what you can find out.

"Christian faith begins with the acceptance that it is normal to appease god with a human sacrifice" anonymous.

Therapy

I would say that the majority of those that have truly been able to put aside their traumatic past with the Jehovah's Witnesses would advise anyone pulling away from the organisation to go and seek counselling.

Trauma is a deep psychological wound. You wouldn't leave any other sort of open wound to rot, fester and go untreated.

It is too easy to make light the experience you have gone through. Many people spend years sometimes never recognising their past trauma with the Jehovah's Witnesses until one day out of the blue, something triggers that trauma and they find themselves shocked that it still has some control of them. Anyone that still has anger, hatred and fear over their past experiences, has not been able to yet face that trauma fully.

On the other hand, you may find that you are constantly down, tearful and lonely, struggling to make friends because you feel so alien to the outside world.

Don't underestimate what you have suffered. Many counsellors believe that trauma experienced from a high control religion triggers Post Traumatic Stress Disorder (or PTSD) and has huge ramifications for your longtime mental health.

I honestly thought that for a couple of decades I had control over my past and what I had suffered. I thought that I had managed to accept it and had moved on. I still found myself angry at the Witnesses and the way my former friends and family had treated me. I had spent years "mourning" them as I was as good as dead to them unless I returned. But the trauma was still there and had not been properly faced and dealt with so it still manifested itself in manic depression and huge waves of anxiety, which led to all sorts of strange and severe illness like symptoms.

Counselling and mental therapy is difficult to accept and yet it is vital to any sort of recovery and to give context to what you have been through. These are not overnight fixes, sometimes therapy can take years. But mixed with research and love from friends, there is an incredible life just waiting for you to go and grasp. The world itself is still a beautiful, fascinating and amazing place. You have the freedom and ability to become and do anything you want, just about. If you want to become the leader of a country or the richest person to ever have lived, erm, that might be a little bit more difficult, but anything else...

You have had several years being heavily controlled and programmed. Breaking that code and getting free of the programming takes time. You will keep finding yourself fighting and being reluctant to accept some viewpoints and that is quite natural. There are many people that refuse to ever open their eyes to the majority of what they believe is their reality. That is the same in the organisation and in the outside world.

Most people have a very narrow vision and are indoctrinated. You may find yourself on a path to being quite free from a lot of indoctrination. You may get to a point where you manage to throw off your deep programming and once you do, you may realise how much everyone else is stuck in these silos of belief. To be outside of those silos can be quite frightening but also quite liberating. You are in quite a unique position, because you have experience in the world that is quite rare, an experience that if used as a basis for wisdom can be a powerful tool in helping others and just bettering your own spirit.

"Looking back spiritually, the Jehovah's Witnesses should have felt 100% loving, upbuilding, making an effort to build family life (not tear it apart), it should have allowed people to reach their potential in creativity, abundance or work for humanitarian causes they enjoy doing.
It's never too late though to leave an abusive cult and to break a cycle in your life or the cycle in your family tree. You never know who you can motivate for someone else to live a better and more authentic version of themselves. I wish all humans that survive an abusive relationship or organization to find purpose, love, joy and blessings in their life."

Natalie Grand – Comic Book Author

Language!

You are going to find that you will have to re-adjust your understanding of some language, both regular and unregular. Here are a few simple examples:

Apostate

This simply means a person that no longer follows a particular faith. You know how different that is from the Jehovah's Witnesses version of this word. It carries so much weight, so much anxiety and controls nearly all ex-Jehovah's Witnesses even decades after leaving the organisation. Most defend the Witnesses almost subconsciously as though even one negative word about the faith or the organisation will still bring retribution even years later. Current Jehovah's Witnesses will call you this regardless of your actions. Personally, I try and own the word. Use it to mean free, open and from a viewpoint of love instead of duty.

Truth

I have written an entire book on this one word. Even people who associate with the Witnesses either through family or perhaps friends at work, pick up that word and call the organisation "The Truth". Of course, to all Jehovah's Witnesses, The Truth is binary, clearly black and white, a simple word that means the organisation and the reality of being a part of it. The more you learn about the flaws of personal perception, the limited inputs and knowledge our brains generally hold and the amount we rely on the faith from our peers, the more you realise that truth is very subjective. Two people can stand right next to each other, watch the same

same incident happen before them and then relay two totally different stories. Truth is very subjective and everyone insists that their truth is the actual reality. Go find your own truth.

Spiritual

For all Jehovah's Witnesses this just means being Christian and feeling the power of god and of the congregation and the organisation. That is such as limited view of spirituality. You can be spiritual without a belief in god. We have two hemispheres of our brain. One is mathematical, logical, measured, sized, quantified and calculated. It requires "proof", something that can be analysed, reasoned and argued. The other side of our brain, we as humans tend to think of as heart, is about faith, networking, connecting, believing, loving, spirituality, god and the universe. Some people have brain damage which throws them totally into either one side or the other. We call these people ill, brain damaged and poorly. Yet in the western world we are obsessed with spending all our time focusing on just the one side of our brain. That is why a lot of society in the outside world struggles with Spirituality. Spirituality can be connecting with the rest of the universe and with people with love and respect, it doesn't have to be that narrow vision of faith and god. Personally, I think we all need to try harder at getting the balance with both sides of our brain.

God

When someone asks me if I believe in god, I always find that a very blinkered view of the word. Christians are the worst for having a very binary vision of what god is. The West has an image that is used by the Watchtower a lot (and is extremely racist) of a pale skinned, middle aged, white bearded man, with full luscious white flowing hair, living amongst the white clouds like some Aryan race's wet dream. As always with a controlling religion, the image is so transfixed with the word "god" that there is no other conceived use of the word, except for perhaps "false god". False god is when your image is not the same as my image for the same guy living up in the clouds. To use our language properly, anything can be a god. God is what anyone worships or follows. Some make gods out of cars, or wealth, some make gods out of people, peers, heroes, some worship money and greed. Some people like to live their lives devoted to work. But you can also use the word god as the universe, as existence itself, as reality or as a collection of every molecule in this and every reality. When someone asks you if you believe in god, they are really asking about a very small view of their own world and asking if you have that world in common, but the use of the language is distorted, heavily filtered and bias.

Worldly

From within the organisation this word has a whole meaning wrapped around "those others". It so negatively used. In fact, it's quite frightening how it is used in the language of the organisation. Basically, anyone who isn't a Jehovah's Witness is a worldly person. They belong to the "other", the Non-Witnesses, the non-human, the ones that will die, the ones that will not be saved and the ones that will be killed in the biggest act of genocide since the story of the flood. Apart from the fact that all practicing Jehovah's Witnesses relish the "coming apocalypse", they cannot wait to build a new world on the bones of 7 billion innocent human beings, potentially on the bones of their own family. This word is used to dehumanise everyone that isn't a Jehovah's Witness. This is a dangerous use of the language because it prepares its followers to not see those that will die as the same as they are. They are lesser. This is the same misuse of language used to convince whole nations that other human beings can then be abused, tortured, ridiculed, beaten and shot. This was the language used to abuse "coloured" people. It is the language used to kill Jews in death camps. Witnesses hope that god will do the killing for them, to ease their

conscience, but what if in the last of the last days, the governing body asks of its followers to take up arms against those worldly people. I think you would be horribly surprised how many dedicated Jehovah's Witnesses would take that invitation up with glee if it hastens the end and their path to paradise.

No part of this world

If Jehovah's Witnesses are really no part of this world, wouldn't you be able to spot them in public without fail? Wouldn't they wear different clothes, wear their hair differently, have totally different values when it comes to style, homes, vehicles, watches, tv's. Wouldn't every aspect of a Jehovah's Witnesses life be so different from the world around it that everyone could point and say, "that is most definitely a Jehovah's Witness". But you can't. Perhaps when they go from door to door, although they look the same as salespeople. Perhaps when they stand next to the carts on the high street do they look uniquely like Jehovah's Witnesses, but isn't it the big sign that says Watchtower that gives it away, not how they look? Jehovah's Witnesses really aren't "not of the world" at all. Everything a Jehovah's Witness does or wears has to be acceptable to the local society so that it "doesn't bring reproach". The organisation doesn't want you to be different, to stand out, to not belong in the local society, they don't want you "bringing attention to yourself". So how is that being "No part of this world"? They are stuck in a 1950's Americana ideal, a fantasy of a nuclear age family that only existed on sitcoms and TV soaps. The language is so distorted.

"You were taught hatred and told it was love. Everything that feels comfortable is unhealthy. Touch your fear."

Micah Allen Losh - Author of the Apostasy Trilogy

Homosexual

Did you know that in the ancient Greek language there is no word for homosexual? The very language used to write the New Testament of the bible, does not have a word that describes homosexuality. So how does the bible manage to say that it is wrong if it doesn't have a word to describe what homosexuality is? That is a very good question, and you don't even have to use Non-Jehovah's Witnesses publications to find the real truth. The bible translation app that the organisation provides can show you the true Greek word used where homosexuals are mentioned in the New Testament. Go and look it up, then look up what that Greek word used and what it actually means, and it isn't homosexual, just simply any sinful sexual act.

Swearing

Swear words are just language. I found that many people in the congregation used to used replacement words instead of swearing. This I always found funny, because isn't that against the spirit of not swearing? Truthfully, the problem with swearing is the subtext behind it and not the words themselves. If any words are used to hurt or throw anger at someone, then surely it's not the words themselves which are the problem. As with a lot of these word examples, the ban on swearing is more about public acceptance than the actual act itself. That 1950's Americana style of fashion and living doesn't like the use of swearwords, the middle-class bible belt of America doesn't like swearing, so swearing is not allowed (in very much the same way as beards are a problem for men and full-time working is frowned upon for women). The problem then arises when you leave the Jehovah's Witnesses and all you hear in the outside world is swearing. There will be a great temptation to fit in. I have known quite a few ex-Jehovah's Witnesses swearing a lot and it sounds just weird. The reason for that is, that we just aren't very good at it really. When an ex-Jehovah's Witness swears, it almost sounds like a four-year-old child that has picked it up for the first time. Context very much matters when swearing. You may think you sound cool, but actually it's quite funny and cringey at times. In my humble opinion, swear words are wonderful and powerful. The more they are used though, the less powerful they become. If someone swears all the time, it loses the potency and becomes a set of words like "erm" that just become pointless fillers. If you save them for when you really need them, they can be so fucking powerful!

Regret

One unfortunate truth you may find difficult to digest is facing up to the decisions you made as a former Jehovah's Witnesses. As you grow outside of the organisation and new realities and other truths open up to you, as well as giving yourself a hard time for not seeing the organisation and the faith for what it was, you may deeply regret some of your actions and decisions as well.

You may have shunned close friends and relatives. You may have been strongly homophobic. You may have treated the opposite sex very poorly or allowed things to happen to you which now you wouldn't allow. Former Elders carry so much more guilt as they took those decisions and biases even further. In some way, we all would have negatively affected other people's lives in our ignorance. But don't blame yourself. At some point you will need to appreciate how clever and total the control over you was. The lure of better things, the altering of your thought processes that you were doing things under the guise of love, and the oppression of your personality and your ability to clearly reason, are the fault of the Jehovah's Witnesses organisation and not yours.

What really matters, is what we do with all those experiences. A negative experience not used for wisdom and greater understanding and empathy, is an experience wasted. The trauma you have faced and will need to face, will be wasted fuel if not used in a more wiser and positive way going forward. You have had a unique life that you share with just a few others around the world. That gives you a unique and specialist wisdom and understanding. It can and will mould you into a much greater human being if you let it. You can become a bright light of hope for thousands of others and anyone else that has suffered any trauma at all in their lives.

Don't look back on your decisions and your former persona as a mistake. I defy anyone to have done any differently under the same circumstances as your own. You could only do and react with what knowledge, experience and the freedom you had at the time. In the same situation, under the same circumstances and with the same wisdom, you would make the same decisions. None of them are mistakes if we learn from them and improve our environment.

"The one thing that you can't take away from me is the way I choose to respond to what you do to me. The last of one's Freedom is to choose one's attitude in any given circumstance."

Viktor E. Frankl, Holocaust Survivor

Falling into another cult

It is hard to accept that the Jehovah Witnesses are a cult. As with all things, this can just be a matter of opinion. Only you can decide what you think the organisation is. Just try and form that opinion after doing your own independent research.

There are many writers and researchers that have tried to define what a cult is. Some researchers even produce signs and models of how to spot a cult and its behaviours. Steven Hassan talks about the B.I.T.E model, a set of clear signs as to whether an organisation is a cult.

Cults do not have to be religious. They can easily be any group of people that has a controlling element. But once you see some of the patterns of a cult, you start to see those patterns everywhere. If you resist accepting that there are manipulative and controlling groups and organisations, you are more likely to slip accidently back into another one.

It's a difficult situation to be in. To accept that the Jehovah's Witnesses are a cult, fits heavily into the acceptance of what the organisation would call the words of an apostate. It's quite clever and one of the signs of a cult, when you fear or struggle to accept what they are because of the consequences of that discovery. You fear to become an apostate by defining the organisation as a cult, so you don't and that leaves you vulnerable.

When you find yourself outcast and ex communicated from your tribe, the loss is

"This is my simple religion. There is no need for temples; no need for complicated philosophy. Our own brain, our own heart is our temple; the philosophy is kindness."

14th Dalai Lama

unbearable and subconsciously, the first thing you will want to do is go and find another tribe. There really is no problem in finding a tribe. It is comforting. We are naturally social creatures and there is safety in the likeminded and in greater numbers. You can easily feel like a gazelle out on the plains, separated from the herd, alone and extremely vulnerable to predators. But sometimes in that state we don't see the predators that are dressed as friends, especially if we still don't recognise the signs from the organisation we have just become free from.

A workplace can be very cult like. People throw themselves into work. They start to talk the business language, fit into the all the cliches, the dress, the talk, the add-ons, the car, the business card, the mobile phone, the predatory body language, the self-improvement programmes, the work functions. At work there can be the struggle to accept others that don't want to fit the businessperson model, the stepped hierarchy, the inability to see any other life outside, the bullying, the excommunication and the subsequent shunning, the inability to really question openly. All signs that point to a cult being formed.

As with a lot of the contents of this book, awareness is key to being properly informed, this book is not about telling you how to lead your new life and how to use your new found freedom. Keep your eyes open to the patterns of another cult and use the wisdom you have earned to at least make your decisions your own. Beware of being manipulated and, also, please always treat others with love and respect.

Recognising a cult is to hold power against it.

"My philosophy is that not only are you responsible for your life, but doing the best at this moment puts you in the best place for the next moment."

Oprah Winfrey

Freedom

Hopefully soon you will realise that you have a freedom that you haven't had before. It's a bit like leaving home for the first time. Suddenly you can do anything in the world that you want to do. The problem is, working out what you want to do with yourself and what to do with your life.

The natural reaction is to go absolutely wild, not just because you can and not just because you want to rebel against everything that you have been stopped from doing for years, there is another element at work in your psyche. It is no small thing to lose everything. You may well think that you are isolated and alone. You may still believe that because of your choices that you are going to die soon at Armageddon so "what the hell, let's just go for it".

You are just like a spring, restricted and fastened up so tightly that the instinct is to just let go and bounce straight into the highest of highs. You may be so desperate to escape from your current mental bindings that you feel desperate to just do it all.

Drink, drugs, sex, gambling, tattoos, screaming, violence, clubs, dancing, riches and a thousand other things that you may want to do simply because you were never allowed to do any of them before. The number of times I have heard people say that they must make up for the time they lost or the childhood they never had or the sexual conquests they would have naturally had or all the youthful experimentations that were not allowed.

It doesn't matter how old you are, you still have a lifetime to explore those things. Going crazy with desire right from the starting blocks, could mean you could miss out on so much as well. Imagine you got arrested and then ended up without any more freedom. You could get back at the organisation and go out and get the word apostate tattooed on your forehead, but then you could never get a job in order to have money to do so many of the things you could do with your life.

If you want to get arrested, if you want to get a tattoo on your head, then that is the freedom you have, but first take some time to think, plan and take a breath and remember, you have years to fulfil what you want to do with your freedom. Get the tattoo next year when you had some time to think fully if it's what you want to do, your forehead will always be there, to tattoo later when you are sure.
The world is not as bad a place as you

think it is, but that doesn't mean that there aren't still people or other organisations that will take advantage of your naivety. You may find that you are desperate to just fit in and be normal and that, in itself, can get you trapped into a poor decision.

There are so many experiences out in the world to take a part in, but there are so many traps that everyone gets stuck in. We all have some things that will take us and hook us in habits and addictions. Everyone has some things that they just seem powerless to fight against. For some, its gambling, for others its money, or alcohol, or smoking, sex, fitness, weed, hardcore drugs, clubbing, fighting, forums, games. Something will grab a hold of you at some point and get you addicted and hooked. It may make no sense at all, but something will get you. If you're lucky it will be just one or two things, if you're very unfortunate a lot of those things may get you.

I'm not telling you to not go out and explore your life, just to be prepared for the catch. The more you do and the heavier you do it, the more likely you are to be trapped if that is your weakness.

My real weakness was smoking. I never really meant to start smoking, I just wanted to look cool on the rare occasion I went out. I was also rebelling, knowing that before, I just wasn't allowed.

In the space of about three or four weeks, I was constantly smoking. I didn't even notice it. All of a sudden, I found that I couldn't stop. I then spent the next

> **"Going to [University] was a brilliant healing mechanism. The Jehovah's Witnessess took 48 years of my life, they're not having any more - you have to be determined to not let them win"**
>
> **Dr Heather Spooner**

twenty-five years get really annoyed at the control smoking had over me. I just couldn't kick the habit, I just couldn't stop smoking. What is strange is that alcohol has never had that same effect on me. I used to drink loads of alcohol, but it never hooked me for some reason. I could just stop drinking and never bother again. So much so that now, I don't drink at all. It just doesn't have any hold on me. I don't care if I never have an alcoholic drink ever again. Yet even after stopping smoking for five years, I still feel like I could take it up again

The more you explore, the more likely you are to get hooked on something. So just be wary and be wise. Have fun but be cautious. And always remember to do all things with love and respect.

Everyone else has to share this world with you.

Finally, one of the greatest struggles is finding a new moral balance. For years you have had a tightly controlled set of morals placed upon you. Now you don't have any moral restrictions other than the ones you choose to take with you. It is difficult to not be morally judgemental to begin with on everyone you meet. But morals are an interesting concept. Many morals are forms of control. They can do more harm than good. The Victorians always thought themselves as highly moral, but what they actually did was stigmatise anyone that was different and then push the natural urges for experimentation and exploration into seedy undergrounds making them dangerous and taboo. Most things that are taboo come from those with power fearing the things they do not understand and then hypocritically dabbling in them anyway behind closed doors.

How can anything be immoral as long as it doesn't hurt or harm those around you. You could say that exposing a person's fear is harming them, but you cannot live other people's lives for them. Do all things with love and care and find your own path. As with everything else in this book, do your research, draw your own conclusions, just draw opinions from wisdom and reason. More than anything, remember that you are far from alone. There is a whole worldwide community of other Ex-Jehovah's Witnesses that can help and guide you. Go out into the world, explore, have fun, fall in love and please help others that follow after you.

Much Love To You All

Disfellowshipping

This is when a baptised Jehovah's Witness is put on private trial by 3 Elders and judged to be guilty of sins such as sex outside of marriage, apostasy, receiving a blood transfusion or smoking. Once found guilty they are then announced publicly to no longer be one of Jehovah's Witnesses and that announcement is a cue for every other Jehovah's Witness to ignore that person. In order for the guilty person to gain forgiveness and be welcomed back into the congregation, they must attend the Kingdom Hall without fail for months, even years sometimes until they are allowed to be a Jehovah's Witness again.

Shunning

This is the act of ignoring a former Jehovah's Witness, or someone that wasn't baptised but has been found to have done wrong (disassociation) or sometimes just because someone has left the religion. This act of ignoring the guilty is called an "act of love". Every faithful Jehovah's Witness must not talk to, associate with or even eat with the guilty person, even if they live under the same roof. Children as young as 13 have regularly been shunned in their own home by their own parents for months. Marriages fall apart, families get ripped to shreds and ex-Jehovah's Witnesses find themselves going from a state of close intimacy with hundreds of people to no-one overnight.

Quick fire guide for non-Jehovah's Witnesses

Suicide rates

It is no wonder that within the ex-Jehovah's Witnesses community it is rumoured that up to 80 percent of those who leave have seriously considered or have actually tried to commit suicide. It is endemic.

Matriarchy

All Jehovah's Witnesses will try and disagree, but women are second class citizens. No woman is allowed any position of authority or power. If a group of Jehovah's Witnesses gather without a man present, one woman can temporarily put on a headscarf (in an act of apology) to take a prayer or lead a study group, but as soon as a young boy enters the room, that women has to relinquish the lead to the boy. A woman's role is to look after her husband, produce offspring and nurture that offspring in accordance with her husband's direction.

Promotion ladder

Children are expected to get baptised in their teenage years. Girls are expected to find mates and create families. Some may go on to excel in preaching work. Men are expected to take on duties within the congregation, then aspire to be Ministerial Servants, a position of training to then become Elders. If especially spiritual, men are then expected to become Circuit Overseers or even better to go and work in the country's main headquarters called Bethel.

Work

It is not looked upon with favour for women to work. Men should provide for their families, but shouldn't spend any unnecessary time with people of the outside world. Self-employment is generally preferred for that very reason. Education that is deemed unnecessary is avoided. Some home school their children because of that. Extra school activity, College and University are strongly discouraged. For this reason, self-employment tends to be in low skilled work.

Birthdays and Christmas

Jehovah's Witnesses do not celebrate either birthdays or Christmas. They do celebrate weddings and wedding anniversaries. There can be a lot of issues for Jehovah's Witnesses who accept gifts from those outside that do celebrate birthdays and Christmas. Many Jehovah's Witnesses will return or even destroy presents given to them because of this.

Blood

Jehovah's Witnesses do not eat any food that contains blood products and they will not accept blood transfusions even if a medical case is life threatening. In hospital, a Jehovah's Witness may have Elders follow them around "encouraging" them not to take blood or not to allow a dying family member to take blood. Today there are many different blood derivatives and blood volume replacement solutions, but many of these are also hotly contended as unscriptural.

POST SCRIPT

While completing this book, a couple of things occurred to me. The journey of becoming POMO, fully being free, reflecting on one's past and constantly researching and unearthing new discoveries, never truly ends and gives life an interesting twist. In some ways I am grateful to have been a Jehovah's Witness as it has taught me some unintended but valuable lessons, such as always questioning the nature of reality, the nature of truth and how everyone tries to push their truth onto you.

Even this past week I have learnt two new things. The first was something I thought of years ago when I was younger and was one of the questions I never had answered as a young witness and was one question of many that kept me from being sure enough to get baptised. I had forgotten this question until I saw a meme recently which made me chuckle.

The question was about the Ten commandments. The Israelites had escaped Egypt, were on their way to the promised land and god gave Moses the Ten Commandments, written in stone, hard pressed into solid rock by god's own hand. An undeniable record of god's direct wishes that were short and to the point and didn't need any further scrutiny.

Then, when the Ten Commandments were delivered, the Israelites were involved in drunken partying and were worshipping an effigy of god made out of gold. So, what did the leaders of Israel do? They slaughtered and put to death 3000 males in the name of god, proclaiming that it was god's commandment. Only that wasn't

written on a stone tablet by the hand of god, in fact that very stone commandment clearly stated that it was wrong to kill. Instead, this was from the voice of men saying they had to do it because god told them that was his wish.

You could just imagine the bearded figure of god, shaking his head from side to side with his head in his hands in disbelief at the idiocy of those leaders.

The second thing that I heard in a discussion which hit home to me, was why the Governing Bodies over the last 100 years make the decisions they make, why they lie and deceive their followers and what do they get from their positions. It's easy to think as an outsider that it's money and power. But none of them look as rich as the company they run. They don't really have any real possessions to the value of their position.

It occurred to me, during the discussion, that being one of the handful of Governing Body members is only achieved by decades of service, years of climbing the "spiritual" ladder and being "chosen" to be part of it. These are deeply spiritual men, that believe that their entire working history has been purposefully blessed by god. They all think they have been chosen out of millions to be god's mouthpiece on earth. They themselves are gods. Chosen by holy spirit, appointed by Christ.

ANY word said against that, is a word against god himself and, of course, they will defend that absolute right to be a Governing Body member because to not be one would be to deny god himself. That is why every Governing Body member will deny ANYTHING that refutes their right to that position and really do believe, with their every fibre, that their every word is the very word of god himself. So, anything negative is going to just be the devil's work, regardless of how true or how real those things are.

It is the delusion of man that they speak the word of god, even when the truth is stamped in stone right in front of them, they will still believe in their own inner voice and say it is the word of god.

That is Fucked UP!